Signage

McGraw-Hill Book Company / New York St. Louis

San Francisco Auckland Bogotá Hamburg Johannesburg
London Madrid Mexico Montreal New Delhi
Panama Paris São Paulo Singapore
Sydney Tokyo Toronto

Signage

Graphic Communications in the Built World

Charles B. McLendon

and

Mick Blackistone

Library of Congress Cataloging in Publication Data

McLendon, Charles B.
    Signage: graphic communications in the built world.

    Includes bibliographical references and index.
    1. Buildings—United States.   2. Signs and sign-
boards—United States.   3. Graphic arts—United States.
I. Blackistone, Mick.   II. Title
TH153.M39   729   81-6049
                                         AACR2

ISBN 0-07-005740-0

1234567890 HD HD 8987654321

The editors for this book were Joan Zseleczky and Esther Gelatt,
the designer was Naomi Auerbach, and the production supervisor was
Sally Fliess. It was set in Avant Garde by The Clarinda Company.
Printed and bound by Halliday Lithograph.

Dedication

This book is dedicated to all who have been, are,
or may become involved jointly or individually
with the task of providing or acquiring
signage for the built environment,
with a special thanks to members of the
Society of Environmental Graphics Designers
and in particular to Dave Meyer and
Paul Arthur, whose invaluable assistance
is sincerely appreciated.

Contents

Foreword

A little neglect may breed great mischief. . . .
For want of a nail the shoe was lost;
for want of a shoe the horse was lost;
for want of a horse the rider was lost.
—Ben Franklin in *Poor Richard's Almanac,*
1758, from George Herbert's
"Jacula Prudentum," 1640

In 1973, the Special Programs Division of the U.S. General Services Administration (GSA) initiated the first of a number of sign and symbol system demonstration projects to test and evaluate the various concepts, materials, and techniques which comprised the current state of the art for graphic communication as related to federal facilities.

On a nationwide basis, GSA was responsible for an inventory of nearly 10,000 buildings, which represented a net occupiable area of approximately 230 million sq ft accommodating over 815,000 employees.

By the end of 1976 ten projects had been completed at a cost of nearly a million dollars and an average lapsed time of almost a year for each. A comparative study of these furnished data that led the program coordinator to the conclusion that it had become not only necessary but also eminently practical to establish uniform criteria in the development and implementation of a flexible standard signage system for use in all federal office facilities. In the absence of such criteria, project architects were frequently charged with the responsibility of developing environmental graphic communication, often with only limited professional expertise or direction and, as a result, did not thoroughly solve fundamental requirements. In essence, the "wheel was continuously being reinvented with shapes other than circular."

It was anticipated that development of such criteria would also establish an overall federal image and at the same time support each department's or agency's individual identity.

By April 1977, a request for proposal to develop this concept was formalized and, in due course, a contract was awarded for its performance.

The successful offeror was required to make a detailed postinstallation inspection of all ten demonstration projects and document the evaluation of each project.

From this evaluation, a uniform standard signage system and subsequent manual was developed as a step-by-step process guide for nonprofessional users.

As the graphics designer consultant who brought GSA's initial concept to its present state of development, I am convinced that this work, *Signage: Graphic Communications in the Built World,* will become a singularly valuable contribution to the small but growing genre of signage references.

Dave Meyer, SEGD

Preface

The world was so recent that many things lacked names, and in order to indicate them it was necessary to point.

—Gabriel Garcia Marquez,
One Hundred Years of Solitude

Preparatory to writing this book, the authors' review of available published material on graphic design for the built environment, and extensive discussions with various members of the design and construction community, revealed that little attention has focused on the development of a working methodology that could equally serve both the practitioner and the user of environmental graphic design.

Designers and teachers of design, contractors and contract administrators, owners, lessors, and building managers and operators who were consulted about the subject matter, the state of the art, and the new directions open to the design and construction industry all echoed the authors' conviction that the entire building community needs to face the challenge of implementing the principles of signage.

In a time when international travel is commonplace and building owners and operators all over the world are opening their doors to millions of visitors, the designer's role, more than any other, grows more influential and necessary. Ironically, throughout the world today, many architects and designers seem unsure of their present role and even more unsure of their future. They are constantly analyzing the marketplace, and the demands that their clients are placing on them, to find their proper "fit."

While several design firms within the United States, Canada, and Europe have provided their clients with effective signage systems, the design and construction industry in general has been reluctant to take the initiative in developing this field of communication despite a growing awareness among architects and designers that they can no longer be satisfied with the status quo. With client demands and responsibilities evident, many professionals are being convinced that if they do not assume active roles in the building community they could be abandoned and replaced by more progressive individuals.

Signage can be regarded as a discipline of its own. It identifies a field of graphic communication that has, in less than 15 years, progressively developed into several recognized professions. However, as with any new concept, it has taken time for signage to spread its influence and illustrate its need. In Europe, for example, the need to bridge the communication barriers, inherent in their multilingual state, resulted in the formation of the International Organization for Standardization (ISO). This organization was formed to pursue the standardization of industrial and transportation-related symbol-signs which have proven to be so vital to international commerce.

Inspired by the Europeans' progress, Canada, in 1970, began to develop national bilingual standards for use in all provincial government business, buildings, and transportation-related applications. And recognition of the potential value to the built environment of this "new" concept in visual communication inspired the U.S. government to sponsor several design studies calculated to produce a unified standard signage system that would serve as a cost-effective management tool for the federal government.

Toward this end, the U.S. General Services Administration (GSA) sponsored a project which was undeniably ambitious for an initial undertaking. It encompassed bilingual signage for all major border crossing stations, which serve more than 270 million people who annually pass through these points along the borders between the United States and Canada and the United States and Mexico. When completed in 1974, this effort received high praise from both neighboring governments.

It is important to note that, since 1974, more than 15 new federal buildings throughout the United States have been designated as demonstration projects for various material/technique applications of signage systems. (See the appendix for postinstallation evaluation information.)

Activities are constantly germinating in the area of signage systems. Designers worldwide are beginning to take a serious look at their responsibilities for developing signage as an integral part of their environmental graphics programs. Similarly, the contractors, building owners, and operators of all facilities are beginning to recognize and identify with the need for signage systems in their structures. All professionals have a well-defined responsibility for the inclusion of effective communication systems in their facility/management plans. The demand for more effective graphic communication techniques is international, and now is the time for environmental graphic designers to initiate their specialized contributions.

Professional concern for the continuing development of more cost-effective quality is the paramount ingredient of true progress. Every change coming into the building business will make operations faster, bigger, and more complex. The products of this progress won't be better, however, unless an increasing number of professionals continue to take their place in the building process.

With this in mind one must recognize that there is a very real chance that the harmonious and human qualities of good design could be sacrificed to speed and economy. But it need not be this way. Sensitivity can coexist with efficiency. If all members of the building community—architects, designers, engineers, general contractors, building owners, and operators—recognize their clients' needs and understand the true nature of the construction industry and the demands placed upon it, they should not find it difficult to locate a place of their own in its future.

Signage: Graphic Communications in the Built World is presented in four major parts and serves as a guide and reference tool for the coordination of the diverse disciplines involved with providing signage for the built world. It is written to inform, instruct, and assist beginning and established professionals interested in the concept, design, fabrication, installation, and evaluation of sign and symbol systems which are applicable to any and all facilities. It is a starting point for professionals who want to meet the demands and requirements of environmental graphic communication.

Part One addresses the art of signage and its "fit" into the building industry. It identifies professional disciplines and defines their roles and interdependence in a total team concept.

Part Two develops the signage system concept and the process and design guides for solving both common and unique design problems.

Part Three presents procurement guidelines and elements for the development of a contract package.

Part Four supplies a summary of the data base, credit notes for selected reference material, identification of information sources, and an index.

During the preparation of the manuscript much study was given to the types of information which would afford each of the "building team" members the greatest understanding and appreciation of the heretofore unrelated special skills essential to successful and cost-effective solutions to signage problems.

The manuscript has been organized in the sequence through which most signage requirements will be ultimately satisfied. The format will allow the user to select the item or items needed to meet specific requirements, whether they be for replacement items, additional items, or a totally new system. Not every sign or symbol will be appropriate for every facility. However, application of the information, as intended, will enable the users to meet their needs by selecting items from the catalog of signs, wherein each is cross-referenced to related specifications and design intent drawings.

Charles B. McLendon
Mick Blackistone

About the Authors

CHARLES B. McLENDON has a background of experience in all facets of graphic design and graphic communication. He was directly involved in the development of graphic standards for WS-4616, the Navy Department's technical publication "bible," and also served as Signage Program/Project Coordinator for the General Services Administration. He currently runs his own consulting firm, Applied Semiotics, in Silver Spring, Maryland.

MICK BLACKISTONE is the owner of M. S. Blackistone and Associates, a public relations/government relations consulting firm in Annapolis, Maryland. He has more than ten years' experience working for the U.S. Senate and the U.S. General Services Administration's Public Buildings Service, where he served as a writer and liaison officer for the design and construction industry.

PART ONE

Program/Project Organization

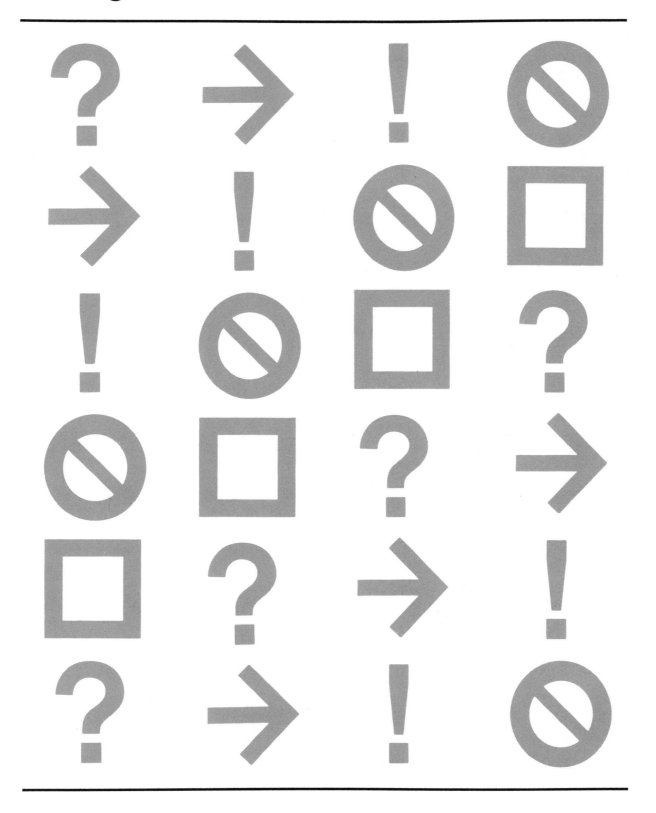

CHAPTER ONE

The Team Concept

There are works which wait, and which one does not understand for a long time; the reason is that they bring answers to questions which have not yet been raised; for the question often arrives a terribly long time after the answer. —Oscar Wilde

When primitive human beings first drew crude pictures on cave walls as a means of self-expression or representation, they initiated a practice that would prove vital to their continued evolution. At the same time they had unwittingly taken their first decisive step on the path of civilization.

Not only had they stumbled upon a means of expanding communication beyond grunts, growls, and gestures, they had also initiated a form of communication wherein every significant milestone of their inexorable progress to the present era would be reflected.

The pace of natural evolution is exceedingly slow, and although human beings eventually managed to develop crafts and commerce, and to build towns, cities, empires, and nations, their modes of communication during this period had undergone little real improvement. Recognizing this condition as a threat to further progress, the ancient Egyptians refined existing picture writing into a fundamental syllabic system of hieroglyphs and ideographs. Foreseeing the tedium inherent in the Egyptian system, the Phoenicians and, in turn, the Greeks and Romans went a step further by developing their system of characters to represent the separate sounds of their spoken language.

Although character forms in many alphabets used today differ from those of the English-Roman, the underlying principle of graphic representation of oral sound is common to most. And the modern English alphabet, despite its imperfections, is recognized as one of the greatest achievements of the human mind, having played a significant role in the growth of modern civilization as we know it.

All over the world, the machine age dawned suddenly and with great impact. Communication modes that human beings had acquired over their half-million years of trial and error needed to be examined and reevaluated. Old concepts of communication that could not be revised to support the industrial revolution were replaced with new communication concepts. As a consequence, new fields of science, engineering, and technology were opened and research and development accelerated until each distinct discipline developed its own vocabulary and attracted its own coterie of professional specialists.

Human beings have now come full circle from their earliest cave days. The natural shelters of their beginnings have been replaced with built environments of such vastness, variety, and complexity that the formation of a new discipline has become necessary to provide ready identification of and accessibility to every defined activity and space between, around, and within each modern manufactured residential or commercial dwelling.

Beyond dictionary definition, "communication" is the art, act, or fact of conveying information from one entity to another. This process can be either active or passive, conscious or subliminal, but in all cases it requires transmission and reception—and, of course, comprehension. Of the many modes now available to us, the most prevalent means of communicating are auditory or visual or a combination of both. Our concern here is with the visual mode, specifically, *environmental graphic communications*.

Prior to the 1950s, graphic communication had traditionally included almost everything that was drawn, painted, or written and distributed to the masses.

More than anything else, outdoor advertising, with its ever-increasing visual dominance along streets and roads, triggered the realization that such two-dimensional signs had reached, and possibly exceeded, the limits of their usefulness and that a new, second generation of signs and sign concepts was urgently needed.

Although attempts have been made by both transportation and industrial planners to develop standards for the application of graphic communications to their needs, it was not until the late 1950s and early 1960s that these early efforts began to coalesce and emerge as new forms of communication technology specifically directed to the built environment all over the civilized world.

Thus, to the consideration of length and breadth, a third dimension of the graphic environment—depth—was added, and environmental graphic communication, or signage, became recognized as a new necessity.

During the past 20 years many new technologies, materials, applications, and processes have been developed throughout the industry, and these activities have given rise to some entirely new concepts and disciplines.

It is important to note that graphic communications is divided into two general areas: One is characterized as performing a people-to-people function, i.e., publications, illustrations, posters, advertisements, and other printed, projected, or broadcasted material. The other, with which we are concerned, is characterized as performing a people-to-people environmental (place) function, i.e., direction, identification, information/orientation, regulatory, and warning/restrictive signs. As urban growth patterns and growing construction budgets and needs are analyzed, this mode of visual communication becomes critical in managing major facilities throughout the world. Although the two areas are quite different in their scale and application, they both depend upon fundamental principles of design for their expression and functional/aesthetic fulfillment.

There are many schools of graphic design, ranging from the elementary and commercial through the college and university levels, which turn out dedicated and competent design practitioners. However, few if any of these schools have yet made more than a token reference to this new field of specialization: graphic communications in the built environment.

When established members of the environmental graphics design profession were polled, the overwhelming majority admitted with pride that their abilities in this specialized field were largely self-taught. In fact, for years the design and construction community has had to use its individual talents to fulfill a client's requests for signs and symbols. This clearly indicates that signage communication is one area of the building community where little brainstorming has been done, on a collective basis, to solve the common problems facing all participants.

Today, because design technologies have developed beyond an individual's ability to apply all of them meaningfully to a project, it has become imperative that the professional expertise each individual has developed and demonstrated be joined to meet the common challenge.

It must be noted that in almost every well-organized, successful endeavor, awareness of the value of team efforts over a "one-on-one" individual effort has been accepted and adopted. In the broad field of design and construction, into which signage is the newest entrant, the programming and establishment of interdisciplinary project teams have consistently proved their value in real and tangible achievement. This point is emphasized because what a firm or individual does with a product, idea, or technique is part of an additive, evolutionary process which, in sum, defines the industry. Similarly, actions cannot be independent when it comes to fulfilling a demand for signage. These actions must be coordinated. True, they will conflict and cancel as often as they reinforce each other. But if each professional works with his or her colleagues to contribute individual special abilities toward common objectives, it should result in an industrywide consciousness and acceptance of this new building discipline.

Although most of this text and most of the illustrative examples relate to contemporary design considerations, signage requirements for traditional and historical restoration projects, malls, industrial parks, and so on can be equally satisfied within the basic signage systems concept which is addressed to all of these facilities. It should meet most of the informational needs and communication requirements of their tenants and visitors. Signage is a universal concept and can be applied to any project through a systems process where the only differences are in the actual end products.

As this system concept is developed, differences among the various markets' signage requirements will emerge. Significant differences will be generated by distinctive user needs far more frequently than from a difference in procurement procedures.

If obstacles exist to cooperative efforts between specialists in the design/build community and specialists in management, these obstacles can probably be attributed to the single basic cause of most problems facing human beings: communication *in absentia*. This does not stem from any reluctance to talk; far from it. It is due to an all too common reluctance to listen.

Once cause is distinguished from symptom, most of the problems associated with signage can be reduced to conversion of concept to implementation, materials and technology to fabrication/installation, and even costs to profitable investments. This can effectively be achieved by following a formula as simple as $A + B = C$; e.g., intelligent talking added to inquisitive listening will produce comprehensive constructiveness. To paraphrase Oscar Wilde, there are many answers which wait and are not understood simply because the fitting questions have not been asked.

Key members of the interdisciplinary team are identified on the team organization chart, Figure 1-1.

Note that Figure 1-1 identifies nonhierarchical areas of responsibility within program management and graphically emphasizes the fact that team members, regardless of rank or seniority, work directly with each other as common input/output needs may dictate.

That any signage effort should be derived from the coordination of many different disciplines cannot be overemphasized. To perform satisfactorily, the project coordinator must possess a broad general knowledge of the skills each member brings to the team and the specific requirements they must meet. The order in which each team member category is introduced should in no way be construed as fixed or inflexible. Nor should the various disciplines imply the total or even a like number of individuals for their performance. As a matter of fact, the fewer the number of decision makers involved on any program/project team at any one time, the greater the economy of time and costs will be in achieving all projected program goals.

In the chart of active team members, most of the professional disciplines brought together are well established in the building profession. The newer ones are graphic design, fabrication/installation, and environmental and social psychology. Technology's rapid growth coupled with diminishing time and finances available to the established practitioner for tapping these new advances, let alone developing skill in their application, have produced, in less than 15 years, these new professions.

Despite the expertise that each member brings to the team, there still may exist a certain naiveté in each with regard to the other's practice. To ameliorate this situation, a brief notation of the applicable skills identified with each major team category is presented. Because the skills and educational backgrounds identified with the fields of management, architecture, engineering, and general construction are well established, only a simple, general definition of these disciplines is presented. The newer additions to the team require somewhat more identification.

Management The collective body of people who develop and administer policy, direct and coordinate resources and activities of many toward specified goals.

Architect/Engineer Combines the classic and modern art of building design with applied sciences of building construction.

Landscape Architect Recommends selection, placement, and care of plants for the built environment.

Space Planner and Designer Lays out space along communication and work flow paths and specifies furniture and furnishings most supportive of intended and designed functions.

Graphic Designer The practitioner in the field of environmental graphic communication has completed a course of study at an accredited school of design. In the course of those studies expert knowledge in the following subjects will have been acquired:

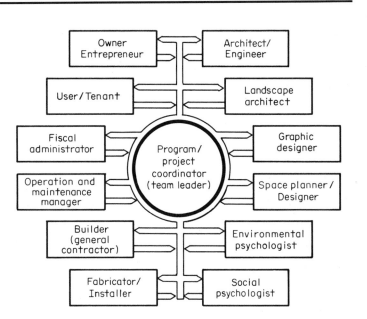

Fig. 1-1 Team organization chart

- Color—its nature and the principles of its use

- Composition, pattern, rhythm and balance, conflict and dominance

- Line, shape, and form; dynamic and static

- Scale and texture

- Typography and semiotics

In the pursuit of the profession, skill will have been demonstrated and talent will have been developed in the application of this individual knowledge.

Social and Environmental Psychologist Provides insights to individual, group, and mass interactions of man with his environment.

Builder/Contractor The general contractor erects the designed facility or alters an existing facility, in faithful compliance to local codes, schedules, specifications, and desires of the client.

Fabricator/Installer The sign system fabricator/installer prepares detailed drawings and specific prototype samples reflecting shop practices in the use of materials and techniques specified for the client by the graphic designer:
- Furnishes all mounting hardware and installs or supervises the installation of all signs comprising the system for the designated site

▪ Develops a manual containing all information pertinent to the care, maintenance, and replacement of any element of the system

In summary, owners, for example, should know what they have to provide for their tenants; landscape architects should know what, where, and how to place shrubbery; architects should know why and where they place a wall or partition, and system engineers should know where all the cables, wires, pipes, ducts, control panels, and boxes will be installed. Graphics consultants who are responsible for signage must not only be aware of these building features but must also coordinate their responsibilities to the tenant with those of the other professional members of the team. It should be understood that every program or project will be unique in both its objective and subjective requirements. At the same time there are, of course, many common elements in problem solving and management responsibility, and each of these can be identified and logically scheduled.

Succeeding chapters deal with all such elements in a detailed step-by-step progression of the decision-making process applicable to implementing practically any signage program. While it is important that a specific mix of compatible specialists be grouped to meet the specific requirements of a given program, the process or methodology for determining the sequence of events in any system will always be the same. Only the end products, the hardware, will be different in their individual characteristics.

Remember: The members of each professional category have attained easily recognized and equally specialized skills in the pursuit of their chosen disciplines. Such skills are the direct result of continued practice in applying established concepts. Talent, on the other hand, can be neither taught, bestowed, nor explained. It is a natural capacity that is as individual as the personality of those who possess it. This aspect is manifest in the total aptness of the end product resulting from its application and should never be confused with purely mechanical dexterity or technical craft. Keep this in mind as you progress through this book. In all cases seek to recognize and combine those skills and talents that will ultimately result in the most successful accomplishment of your signage program.

Once the "team" is assembled, the first order of business should be the development of a program management plan or work flow diagram which will establish program/project elements in priority sequence.

Note: For detail refer to Michigan Council for the

Arts' *Client Guide for Signage & Architectural Graphics* in Part 3.

Subsequent to accomplishing this task, detailed program/project work plans or work progress charts should be developed.

These two chart models (Figures 1-2 and 1-3) represent only basic management considerations. The categories can be expanded, contracted, moved, or even eliminated to fit any specific program requirement.

Figure 1-2 is a simple work flow diagram or program management plan that extends and complements the organization (team) chart.

Figure 1-3 is a variant of the Gantt or bar chart, which lends itself well to single or multiple (composite) discipline identification and task/event scheduling. "Time" can reflect any constant unit— days, weeks, months, or years. Tasks/events should be recorded in the descending order of their scheduled initiation. This also provides an indispensable checklist.

Where performance times overlap, the need for interdisciplinary interaction and coordination is generally indicated.

In each chart, all elements can be expanded to accommodate related subtitles or functions. The detail into which each can be broken is virtually limitless. However, to ensure clarity, simplicity, and manageability, it is strongly suggested that sublevel detail be consigned to keyed charts.

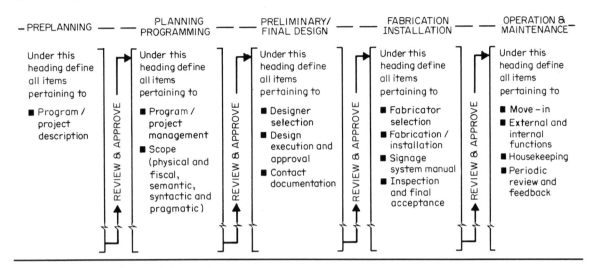

Fig. 1-2　Program/management plan: work flow diagram

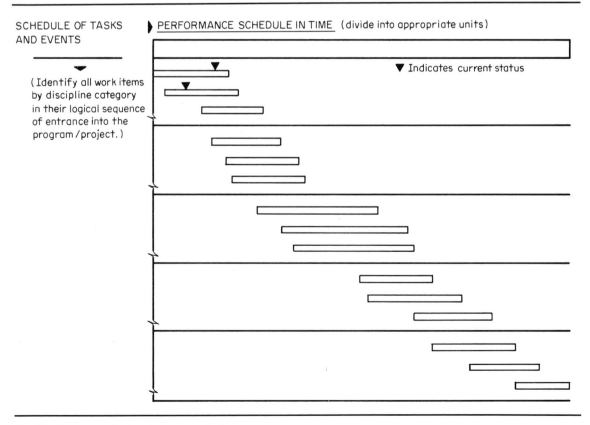

Fig. 1-3　Program/project work progress chart

CHAPTER TWO

Data Base Summary, Vocabulary of Terms, and Classification of Sign Types

It is an understanding of structure and of the intrinsic organization in which structure becomes embedded that is elusive and that has to be worked toward by observation and analysis.
—Dr. Karl Pribram, professor of psychology, Stanford University

While signage programs have been developed on a relatively small scale over the past 15 years, several significant projects were completed in the 1970s. Despite the fact that most of these programs were implemented and evaluated in federal government buildings throughout the United States, the lessons learned can be considered universally applicable.

Of the 10 U.S. installations reviewed and evaluated, only 2 came close to meeting their design intent fully. A pragmatic assessment of the shortcomings, although tangible and correctable, exposed clearly symptomatic characteristics of the problems identified in Chapter 1.

The data produced from the postinstallation evaluations of these "demonstration" projects statistically reinforced the need to develop a uniform methodology for determining and acquiring effective environmental communications (i.e., signage) systems. (See the material on data base in Part 4.)

In this regard, the first item of concern is the unique vocabulary within each discipline; the vocabulary may not be clearly understood by professionals in other disciplines.

To facilitate comprehension of the remaining text, some terms that may not be familiar are defined as follows:

GENERAL

Designer   Any person, whether a professional consultant or on in-house staff, given the responsibility to provide services necessary to design or obtain a sign or signage system for a specific facility.

Facility Self-Protection Plan   A graphic device consisting of a floor plan and emergency evacuation route information relating to stair and exit locations and their use in case of fire or other emergencies.

Referent   The functional concept for which a specific symbol stands.

Sign   A graphic device which conveys specific information or meaning—a *singular, implicit graphic notice* (author's mnemonic device).

Sign System   A discrete graphic system comprising a number of individual graphic devices that are related by common characteristics or properties and arranged to convey all information considered essential to the optimum functioning of a specific building (facility) and its occupants.

Symbol   A graphic device which relies in whole or in part upon simplified pictorial representation.

Symbol-Sign   A graphic device conveying information in whole or in part in symbolic form and consisting of shape, color, and symbol.

DESIGN

Ascender   The stroke of a lowercase letter that extends above the X height.

Cap Height   The height of capital letters.

Counter   The area enclosed by the strokes (face) of the letter.

Descender   The stroke of the lowercase letter that extends below the base of the X height.

Fixed Sign   A sign with a set format; the sign remains constant through all applications.

Font   The complete assortment of type in one size and style.

Graphic   Written, drawn, engraved, or printed words or symbols used to represent or convey meaning.

Graphic Content Description   The approved (accepted) unique verbal description of the graphic elements that constitute the symbol.

Illumination, Direct   A sign for which external illumination is directed onto its face.

Illumination, Indirect   A sign which is illuminated by ambient light; no special means of illumination is provided.

Illumination, Internal   Signs with an integral, internal light source which projects light through the sign face background and/or message.

Margin   The space from the sign panel edge to the limit of the message area.

Message   Pictures or copy at a defined size.

Message Area   The area within the sign panel describing the limits of the message.

Message Grid   The grid employed to establish uniform spacing of letters, words, and lines, both vertically and horizontally within the message area of the sign panels.

Message Unit   Defined message height positioned within a space of any specified number of equal basic grid subdivisions and which includes prescribed space above and below the cap height of the message.

M Height   The optimum height at which a particular sign shall be mounted, measured from the top or bottom of the sign panel to the finished floor or surface grade.

Module   Any unit of measurement established to express proportions.

Pica   The unit of measurement for a line of type; approximately $1/6$ in.

Point   The unit of measurement of traditional type sizes in height; approximately $1/72$ in or $1/12$ pica.

Serif   A crossline that finishes off the stroke of a letter.

Stroke   The stem and curves that form a letter.

Type   A rectangular block, typically of metal or wood, bearing a relief character from which an imprint is made.

Typeface   Identifies both the printing surface and the style of the type character.

Type Family   A group of alphabets linked by style and generic characteristics.

Typography   The practice of arranging letters of a typeface to form words and sentences into an intelligible and aesthetic order.

Variable Sign   A sign which has a changeable format, its size depending upon the legend (message).

Weight   The boldness or thickness of a typeface determined by the contrast of strokes and the proportion between face and counter.

X Height   The height of a straight stroke of a piece of lowercase type without ascender or descender.

FABRICATION/INSTALLATION

Elevation Drawings   Scale drawings which indicate ground-to-roof and/or floor-to-ceiling features and details.

Floor Plan   A scale drawing indicating the area and configuration of the space and building system features of the included floor.

Message Schedule   A sequentially numbered list of all signs in the system arranged in the order of encounter and containing all pertinent (coded) information, such as sign type, message or messages, and quantity, cross-referenced to the sign schedule and sign location drawings.

Mount   The method of securing the sign in a fixed position.

Shop Drawings   Drawings prepared by the fabricator of the intended sign types' material, and construction details for review and approval by the client and designer.

Sign Location Drawings   A set of site and floor plans on which each numbered sign's location is superimposed.

Sign Schedule   A list of all sign types including size, fabrication technique, and mount recommendation.

Site Plan   A scale drawing indicating the extent and configuration of the surrounding land and the location and configuration of the building proper.

CLASSIFICATION OF SIGN TYPES

Because of the complexity of needs and functions which are translated into visual communication problems, solutions should be sought through a systems approach that will provide practical and functional criteria and guidelines with sufficient flexibility to adapt to or include any special requirements.

As a result, the integrated visual communications system will be a logical solution to the direction, identification, orientation and information, and traffic-control requirements of a specific project. Keep in mind that even though tenant and employee turnover generates a constant need for effective, current information properly provided, the public's ability to use and rely on the system will reflect its true success.

Occasionally visitors may be directed by security personnel or a receptionist and may even be met or escorted to their destination. In many instances, however, no control is offered. Consequently, visitors must find their own way to their destination. Where this situation exists, appropriate visual communication will be needed.

This visual communication system can be developed, and it consists of five categories of sign types into which all signs will fall.

These five basic sign types have been coded throughout the book by a series of five easily remembered and easily drawn symbols. They are:

Orientation and Information

These signs provide the user with information about where things are, when offices or shops are open (or closed), and other information of a general nature.

Directions

These are signs which include prominently displayed arrows to direct the user toward something—a room, a shop, a roadway, or a facility.

Identification

These are signs which identify something—an office, a shop, a facility, or a building.

Prohibitory and Warning

The purpose of these signs is to tell the user what he must not do and what he must be careful of, generally expressed in symbols or symbol-signs (symbols combined with words).

Official Notices

These signs display information of an official nature and should not be confused with orientation signs.

Elements that are basic to any successful system fall into three general categories: *graphic*, *semiotic*, and *mechanical*.

Graphic elements include, but are not limited to, format, color, typography, size, symbols,

and lighting requirements, all of which ensure the optimum legibility and readability of each sign in the system. It is important to understand the distinction between legibility and readability. *Legibility* concerns the viewer's physical ability to see a sign and to distinguish letters or color. *Readability* concerns the viewer's ability to perceive a message. Signs must be both legible and readable to function properly.

In order to communicate the intended meaning to the viewer, the choice and arrangement of words conveying the message of signs is critical and should reflect clarity, simplicity, and forcefulness.

Semiotic elements are semantics, syntactics, and pragmatics. In the context of signage, *semantics* refers to the relationship of a visual image to a meaning, *syntactics* refers to the relationship of one visual image to another, and *pragmatics* refers to the relationship of a visual image to the user.

Mechanical elements are hardware components which utilize the latest material, fabrication, and installation technologies available. A balanced application of all these elements will render a "customized" system that will be flexible in use and obtainable within acceptable budget considerations.

PART TWO

The Systems Concept and How to Use It

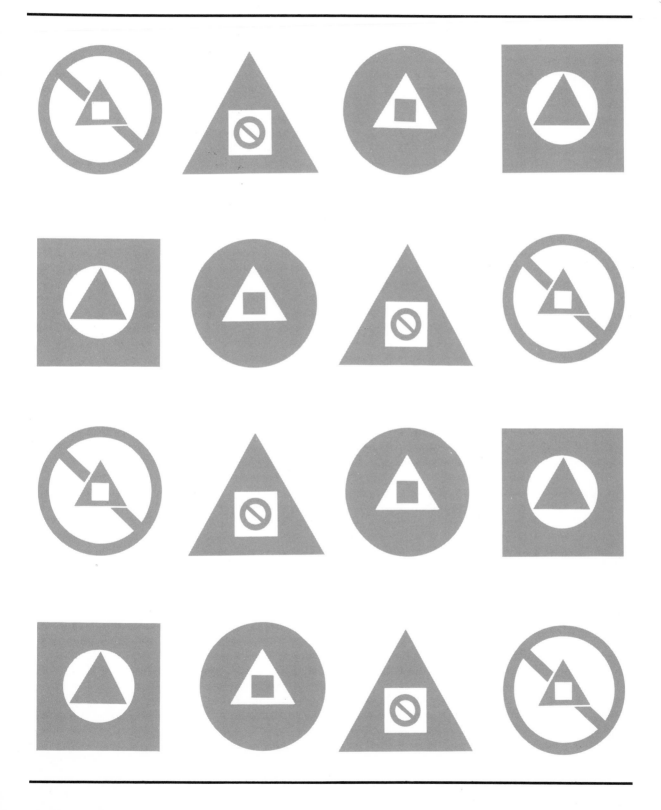

CHAPTER THREE

The First Step

A design is a plan to make something: Something we can see or hold or walk into; something that is two dimensional or three dimensional, and sometimes in the time dimension. It is always something seen and sometimes something touched, and now and then by association, something heard. It is often a single item and just as often a mass produced product.
—Peter Gorb, from Pentagram's
Living by Design
Whitney Library of Design

The design process, in itself, should be characterized as being a system. There are many elements, sometimes seemingly disparate in nature, which comprise the process or the system produced. This section addresses those elements and their application within the sign system concept.

THE SYSTEM SCOPE

The use of a signage system is applicable but not limited to the following markets:

1. Office buildings
   a. Federal, state, county, and municipal government
   b. Commercial
   c. Financial
   d. Industrial

2. Hospitals/medical facilities

3. Schools

4. Transit systems (road, rail, air, water)

5. Libraries

6. Stadiums: sports complexes, recreation areas, and parks

7. Shopping malls

8. National border crossing stations

Design Considerations Cover

Exterior/interior direction, identification, orientation/information, and regulatory devices for vehicular (parking) and pedestrian traffic control.

Of distinct interest and relevance is the 1979 estimate that nonresidential construction in the United States could reach 45 billion dollars, and that the potential signage market portion could reach 400 million dollars. The latter figure was derived from the assumption that every million of population represented 2 million dollars of signage sales, with the largest demand for signage coming from new construction, remodels, and additions.

THE SYSTEM OPTIONS

To ensure general compatibility with many different types of facilities, a number of options within specific areas of a typical sign system are provided. They are:

- Color
- Letterstyle
- Sign panel size
- Materials
- Fabrication details
- Hardware
- Mounting
- Graphic application
- Frame design

In each of these areas, within the framework of analysis and evaluation of the state of the art of sign system design, a number of cost-effective options embodying flexibility, changeability, and maintainability are provided.

THE FIRST STEP IN PUTTING TOGETHER A SYSTEM

When starting a signage system consider the professional qualifications of your in-house personnel first. In most cases, however, there are merits to hiring a specialized graphic design consultant.

Tasks which must be performed and for which the use of a consultant might be considered are:

1. Predesign activities
   - Gather data
   - Evaluate data
   - Facility walk-through
   - Prepare sign location drawings
   - Record messages
   - Selection from catalog of signs

2. Special design requirements

3. Preparation of sign system package
   - General conditions
   - Special conditions
   - Performance specifications
   - Design intent drawings
   - Sign type/specification numbers
   - Message schedule
   - Sign location plans
   - Unit contract list cost estimate

4. System package evaluation

5. The procurement process
   - Solicitation for proposals/bids
   - Contract award

- Fabrication inspection
- Postinstallation evaluation

The design process will elaborate on each of these tasks and provide the necessary guidelines to assist in developing sign system requirements.

Selecting a Consultant

Professionally designed and fabricated signage will help visitors and occupants find their way easily and safely throughout a building, or a complex of buildings, and in outdoor areas. This will be accomplished by presenting identification and directional information in a clear and concise manner.

There are several national organizations and associations of graphic designers and sign fabricators that will assist the nonprofessional in identifying established credible signage services. (See the list of sources in Part 4.)

It is recommended that a list be developed of several graphic designers who can fulfill specific project needs. Look at the work of those reviewed in trade periodicals and books. Check the membership lists of applicable professional organizations and talk to others who have successfully used their services in the local area.

In interviewing graphic designers or fabricators ask to see examples of their past performances. Ask questions about the specific goals and problems that were faced and how they handled them. Ask how they might approach the immediate problem.

The role of the graphic designer, whether an in-house staff member or an outside consultant, requires that a defined format be followed. This will ensure a certain degree of uniformity in the project effort and will serve more efficiently in controlling and evaluating the project's progress and results.

The design process can take many forms and directions. The following will serve as a guide to, and provide required controls for, those items which should be rigidly adhered to and those items which have built-in flexibility. The guidelines and processes should be understood and followed by all nonprofessional, paraprofessional, or professional personnel involved with each project.

By following the guidelines of the design process even nonprofessional personnel will be able to resolve basic signage problems and prepare related procurement documents.

Data Gathering: Who and How

The process of gathering data can be relatively simple if the roles of responsibility are clearly identified and understood. When it has been determined that a facility requires signing, there are certain decisions that must be made initially, i.e., assignment of a program/project manager (coordinator) and identification of user representatives.

Although the sequence of steps for gathering data is not rigid, acquiring a thorough understanding of and familiarity with the facility and receiving proper user input are essential.

Generally, it is recommended that the project manager and designer meet with the building's manager, user representatives, and project architect if dealing with a new facility. They should acquire a knowledge of the facility's human functions such as traffic flow for employee/public use, security, and provisions for the handicapped.

The owner/manager is responsible for clearly informing the users of their responsibility to provide their input early in the project's development.

The objective of this information-gathering activity is to supply the designer with sufficient material and background to perform a facility walk-through with the floor plans and then prepare preliminary message schedules and sign location plans. The designer will subsequently submit these plans back to the users and the building's manager for confirmation and adjustments.

The Tools Needed for Gathering Data

First and most important is a sound understanding of how the facility to be signed works. This will be accomplished through *discussions* with the architect, the users, and the building's manager, and through a thorough comprehension of the facility's plans.

Second is a complete *set of site/floor/parking and area assignment plans,* as appropriate. It is on these plans that the initial sign locations are recorded.

Third is a *supply of preliminary message schedule forms* on which essential bits of information about each sign are recorded.

Fourth is the *Catalog of Signs,* from which the exact sign type for each individual sign location recorded on the plans and message schedule forms can be determined and selected.

With these four basic tools, almost anyone can successfully gather and prepare the required data.

CHAPTER FOUR

The Systems Concept in Action

Architectural lettering cannot be reduced to function in the sense of legibility. Its function is to convey an impression, as well as to spell out words. Also, it is part of a whole, and must be related to the function and design of that whole.
—Nicolette Gray, *AIA Journal*

Specific recommendations have evolved which relate to the concept of visual communications in terms of where signs go, what they should say, and the priorities and hierarchy of how the information is organized.

To present these recommendations, an outline format is used which follows the path of an individual, first in an automobile, then as a pedestrian. In each situation, one or more of the five classifications of sign types is referenced.

SIGNS AND THEIR LOCATIONS

Site →□ Assume that the visitor has arrived at an unfamiliar destination. If it has been effectively signed, the visitor will be guided by means of directional devices containing limited information and arrows.

Parking !⊘→□ The parking lot entrance will be identified with employee and visitor designations along with the facility name. Entrances and exits will be identified with appropriate information for the handicapped. Direction to visitor parking within a lot will be clearly displayed. Other signs included can be:

1. Level identification
2. Exit direction and identification
3. Traffic regulation (DOT)
4. Space designation
5. Limited access, tow-away-zone parking
6. Special instructions/regulations
7. Handicapped parking identification

Generally, all facilities with self-contained parking will display signs that instruct pedestrians to go to the main building lobby directory for full information. This instruction will be located in or near the principal vertical-access facilities—elevators, escalators, or stairways.

Building Identification ! The building will be identified by an identification sign, free-standing or applied to the building's facade.

The primary message of this sign will contain only the dedicated name of the facility. No tenant information will be displayed on this sign. The facility address and/or seal/logotype may be included if required.

Individual facilities located in leased spaces may have all graphic communication requirements outside of the actual leased space provided by the landlord. Graphic communication requirements inside the leased space will generally be provided by the tenant. However, responsibility for such will need to be determined on an individual case basis.

Main Building Directory/Information Center ? Visitors will be directed from parking areas to building entrances and from access floors above and/or below the main entrance level to the main building directory/information center, generally located in the entrance lobby. This directory will list all resident functions alphabetically; the listings will be followed by their location in the facility.

Building floor plans in conjunction with the directory may be considered where it is determined professionally that they help significantly to clarify direction for the user.

Elevators !⊘□ Elevator lobbies on each floor will include floor identification. Some buildings may have elevator floor service designations, such as, "Express Elevator" or "Floors 1–6." Also located at each elevator service area will be notices "In case of fire, use exit stairs. Do not use elevator."

Elevator cabs will display "No Smoking" signs, capacity signs, and elevator number along with an emergency telephone number.

Floor/Corridor Identification ! The need exists for identifying floors at public access points. This may be a plaque or color coding system. Corridor identification may be necessary where the floor plan is complex.

Floor information ? Once the desired floor is reached, the visitor will see the specific floor directory. This will be located within or directly adjacent to the elevator lobby. Visitors arriving at the floor by means of bridges or secondary access will also be guided to this directory.

Interior Directional → Directional graphic devices will guide the visitor from the initial point of entry to the facility to the building directory/information center. A directional device at each floor directory location will guide the visitor to the desired destination. This device will separate each floor according to layout and room numbers and will direct the visitor to each part of each floor. Beyond this location, all directional devices may direct by room number only.

Room Numbering System ! Room numbering should be consistent throughout the facility to promote easy control of visitors and employees. Rooms requiring only a number will utilize the number panel part of the office identification sign or an "inventory room number" device.

Area Identification **!**   Primary area identification will be used to identify a wing or partial floor where there are multiple office or retail functions in that area. Each office or retail function will be listed on this device.

Office Identification **!**   General office identification devices include room number and office function. No individual names.

Entrance into an individual's office from the corridor will include room number and the individual's name or names if more than one individual occupies that office. This will apply only if the individual's name is interchangeable with the title of that office, e.g., *given name—President, Vice President,* etc.

Conference rooms or special-function rooms will be identified with a room number and have provision for a current-activity agenda if required. If an unrelated single-office function happens to be located within a larger office area, the single-office function will have to be listed on the identification sign for the larger area. Its room number will, of course, be the same.

If there are multiple functions within an office, each function will need to be listed at the primary office entrance. All functions will be given the same room number. No names will be listed.

Where a single office has more than one entrance, only the designated main entrance will be identified with a room number and name or function. The remaining doors will be identified with a sequential number only.

If there are four or five offices located within a suite area and there are multiple doors from the corridor into a general secretarial or reception area, the entrance adjacent to the receptionist will be designated as the main entrance. The sign will include room number and related function. All other entrances will have a sequential number only.

If the main office entrance has a controlled reception area, no secondary office identification will be required except by a letter or number designation.

If the primary office entrance does not have a controlled reception area, then secondary office identification will be provided and should include letter or number designation, function, and title of management level.

Open planned space situations will be provided area or function identification for all included office units.

Since it is assumed that leased facility owners will provide signs up to and including lessee's

identification, it is recommended that immediately inside the designated entrance the visitor be exposed to the identification and function presented as an extension of the facility's graphic communication system. This could be done by a panel with graphics applied or by free-floating graphics without background (clear panel).

Other secondary signs supplementing owner-provided signage in leased buildings will conform to the standards for those owned buildings.

Name Plaques **!**   Name plaques may be provided for office personnel. The individual's name, or name and title, may be provided.

Provision is made for both desk-type and office landscape partition-type name plaques.

Egress Control ⊘ → ☐   Egress control devices are required for all buildings, and the development of the specific requirements needs to be coordinated with local accident- and fire-prevention personnel.

Stairs **!**   To assist in emergency evacuation and floor circulation, it is recommended that the inside of stairwells have floor number identification prominently displayed at each level landing.

It is also recommended that all stairs, in addition to existing illuminated exist signs, be identified with "Exit Stair" and graphic symbol. This identification will be located on the corridor side of the door leading into the stairwell.

Rest Rooms **!**   All rest rooms will be identified according to use with symbol designation and, if required, word designations.

Bulletin Boards ☐   This item is provided as an option, to be located at key points of office personnel circulation. Its prime purpose is to provide a standard format and some degree of control over a normally uncontrollable situation of notices, advertisements, etc.

Inventory Room Number **!**   This item provides an economic and unobtrusive method of providing an inventory room number for rest rooms and nonpublic areas determined not to need regular identification. These will be located on an upper corner of the door frame.

Sign System Explanation ☐ An explanation of the sign system should be installed in the building and located in the main lobby. It should contain a brief clarification of room numbering, handicapped access, directory function, and the method of directing people movement. This information should be located in close proximity to or within the building directory.

Signs for the Handicapped ! Refer to the general specifications section on requirements for the handicapped.

HOW TO DEVELOP SIGN LOCATIONS

The question will arise, "How does one determine sign locations?" The recommended method is, again, to assume the role of a visitor coming to the building for the first time and performing a walk-through. Every point along the visitor's path to and throughout the building which requires a decision on the visitor's part must be satisfied by one or more of the five types of signs described in the classification of sign types.

The "facility walk-through" process is recommended as the best way for developing sign locations. Of course, there can be only two conditions which will determine the procedure for a facility walk-through. Either the facility will be existing and physically available, or the facility will still be in its development stages.

If the facility exists, one has the benefit of visually experiencing what happens throughout the facility in relation to potential sign requirements.

If the facility is not yet built or completed, then one must rely on a set of site/floor plans for the initial planning effort.

As one performs a walk-through of the facility one should be able to identify the need for specific signs quickly.

The most effective and convenient way to do this *(and subsequently communicate it to the fabricator)* is to mark the sign locations on a set of blueprints of the exterior and interior of the building using circled numbers. The circled numbers become a series of consecutive sign numbers for use in the procurement document. Start at the site of the facility, leading to parking and/or entrance, then proceed from floor to floor.

Signs are indicated at right angles to the flow of traffic and are identified by a single line for single-faced signs, and a double line for double-faced signs.

At this point in the process concern should be focused only on the type of sign needed at each location, not on its message content.

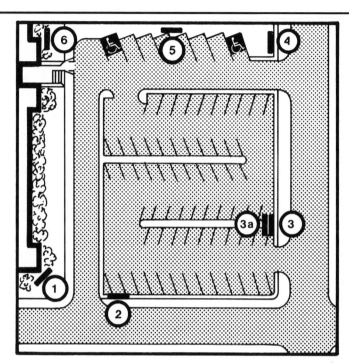

Locating signs on site plan

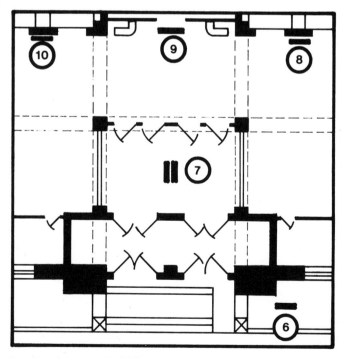

Locating signs on main lobby

HOW TO DEVELOP OUTDOOR SIGN LOCATIONS

Pedestrian signs are, of course, smaller in scale than vehicular signs but the general principles controlling their location are basically the same.

Signs are more effective when located at right angles to the direction of traffic than when they are parallel to it. When locating signs at right angles, the nearest edge of the sign to the pathway or sidewalk should not be closer than approximately 5 ft to inhibit vandalism and damage from other sources.

Identification **!**   When two-way traffic is involved, locate these signs free-standing at right angles to the direction of traffic flow.

When one-way traffic is involved, locate these signs on the building to enhance visibility and inhibit vandalism.

Direction **→**   Directional signs are useful only insofar as they are reliably located to lead the users to the desired destination and are located for maximum effectiveness.

Where an opening or a ramp exists for which directional signs are required, the sign should be located opposite (or over the opening).

Turn signs should be located before (or when more practical, after) the turn.

Orientation/Information **?**   These signs should be located to maximize their effectiveness without causing bottlenecks in the traffic flow.

Prohibition **⊘**   "No Entry" signs should be located on or over doors or other openings where entry by pedestrians is *prohibited.*

Official Notices and Other Information **☐**   These signs are located in the same manner as *orientation* signs. They should be located to maximize their effectiveness without causing bottlenecks in the traffic flow.

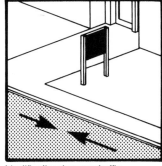

Identification: two-way traffic

Identification: one-way traffic

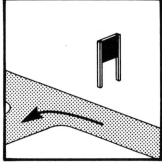

Directional signs

Turn signs

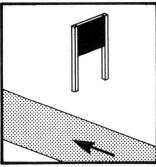

Orientation/information

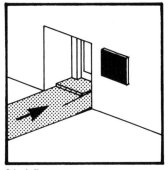

Orientation

Prohibition

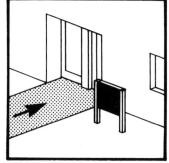

**Official notices and
other information**

HOW TO DEVELOP INDOOR SIGN LOCATIONS

Indoor signs are located on (or sometimes suspended from) building elements. Generally, indoor signs are smaller in scale than exterior signs, since indoor signs are viewed at somewhat closer range.

It is important that these signs be located in a consistent and logical manner that will maximize their effectiveness and keep their total number in the building to a minimum.

Orientation/Information **?** Directories should be located on walls inside the main entrance.

Direction **→** Directional signs should be located wherever the visitor has to make decisions as shown on these diagrams. Four signs are required at "+" intersections and three at "T" intersections of corridors, as shown.

Identification **!** If the identification of a door (or room) is a number only, locate it on the door, but otherwise to the right (or left, if necessary) of it. Locate signs over counters either aligned with the front or centered on them.

Orientation/Information

Direction

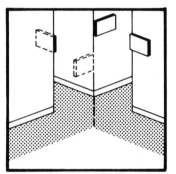
Direction

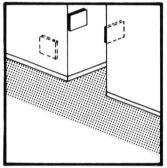
Direction

Direction

Identification

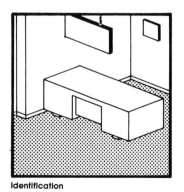
Identification

Prohibitory/regulatory

Prohibition/Regulation ⊘ "No Entry" signs should be located on doors to rooms to which the public has no access. "No Smoking" or other such signs should be located on walls.

Official Notices ☐ These signs should be located on columns or walls where they will be clearly visible to the public when being interviewed by facility personnel.

Prohibitory/regulatory

Official notices

HOW TO RECORD SIGN MESSAGES

The preliminary message schedule forms, on the facing page, will allow the quick documentation of all pertinent information about each sign and, at the same time, provide the groundwork for the eventual contract package message schedules.

The message forms have been designed to simplify the task by providing for check-marking of boxes or filling in of missing information where required. Just as when marking blueprints, the main concern is with noting the need for signs in certain locations. At this point, there is no need to be concerned with the final message as it will appear on the sign. Generally indicate the text of the message.

Procedure

First, mark the sign number that corresponds to the one marked on the blueprint in the circle at the top left corner. (Note that there is provision for two separate signs on each sheet.)

Second, mark the category of the sign that is required: exterior (E) or interior (I), vehicular or pedestrian and orientation, direction, prohibitory and warning, identification or notices and information. (Refer to sign type classification section.)

Third, write down the appropriate rough message and note whether the sign is to be single- or double-faced.

Directional signs always contain arrows, which may point in any one of only eight directions. Refer to the portion on arrows in the general specification section.

Prohibitory messages are generally enclosed in red circles with a red diagonal slash across them. The only exception is the "No Entry" sign. Usually the "No Entry" sign is shown symbolically only (i.e.,

without words). Either place the symbol on the form or put the message in parentheses ( ).

Caution or warning messages are generally enclosed in yellow triangles.

Caution or warning signs usually contain symbols along with words of explanation. Place the words describing the symbol wanted in parentheses ( ), with the words to be expressed below the symbol without brackets. The actual symbol may be illustrated.

If the message block of the sign is to contain only a room number, that's all that is required.

If a description of the office or function which occupies a room is required in addition to the room number, both are noted.

If, for some reason, no room number is needed, the functional description is all that is required.

For official notices, copy the sign number (from the blueprint location plan) and note the category in its respective position. Because these official notices have standard wording with which one is probably familiar, simply identify which notice is wanted by referring to it by name in parentheses.

Preliminary Message Schedule

(1) Sign No.

(2) Classification:

🚗	🚶	E	I
?	→	!	🚫	□

(4) Catalog | Quantity:

Location Plan No.

Mounting:

Message:

(3)

(5) (6)

S/F		D/F		Illuminated		Non-Illuminated	

**Sample preliminary message
schedule form**

Preliminary Message Schedule

(7) Sign No.

Classification:

🚗	🚶 ✔	E	I ✔
?	→ ✔	!	🚫	□

Catalog *INTERIOR DIRECTION* | Quantity:

Location Plan No.

Mounting:

Message:

← G4 - G50
← G200 - G250
← G300 - G355

S/F	✔	D/F		Illuminated		Non-Illuminated	✔

**Completed preliminary message
schedule form**

CHAPTER FIVE

The Next Step:
Components of the System

Basic to the understanding of signage systems is the reduction of the whole problem into its components, precise identification of them and from them, assembling a system that will work.
—Paul Arthur

When the preliminary message schedule for a project has been completed and put into chronological (facility walk-through) order, a search of the catalog of signs should provide the range of sign types that will satisfy most needs. An illustration of each item in the catalog is cross-referenced to a corresponding design intent drawing and related specification.

It is quite possible, however, that certain requirements cannot be satisfied within the limits of the catalog and the designer must, therefore, provide a design effort to satisfy these special needs. In this case, a decision must be made on whether to perform the design effort in-house or solicit the assistance of a professional consultant.

In making this decision the extent of participation by either professional must be determined, i.e., to provide special design needs only, or to complete the balance of the project. In either event the following outline lists the tasks which must be accomplished by the design professional.

1. Prepare contract package
   - General conditions
   - Special conditions
   - Performance specifications
   - Design drawings
   - Sign type/specification numbers
   - Message schedule
   - Sign location plans
   - Unit cost estimate
2. Contract package evaluation
3. The procurement process
   - Solicitation for proposals
   - Contract award
   - Fabrication inspection
   - Installation inspection
   - Postinstallation evaluation

For federal government sign system procurement each of the regional offices of the U.S. General Services Administration (GSA) will make available copies of the elements required for preparing and issuing a successful contract package for the procurement and installation of signs. (See the list of sources in Part 4.)

These elements include:

   - General conditions and notice to bidders

   - Special conditions

   - Specifications

   - Design drawings

   - Message schedule forms

   - Grids for sign layouts

The following is an outline of bid specifications for single items or a total system of elements applicable to both government and commercial procurement. Further information will be found in the sections on specifications and design intent drawings in this book.

1. Exterior signs
   a. Item identification (building identification)
   b. Sign panel or panels
      (1) material
      (2) size/quantity
      (3) graphic application
      (4) thickness
      (5) single- or double-faced
      (6) color
      (7) finish
      (8) sign panel edges finish
   c. Typography/art
      (1) style and size
      (2) upper- and/or lowercase
      (3) position (flush left or right)
      (4) color
      (5) message (include message schedule form)
      (6) letter/word spacing
   d. Sign supports
      (1) material
      (2) color/finish
      (3) size
      (4) length-above grade
   e. Mounting hardware

2. Building/floor directories
   a. Item identification
   b. Directory
      (1) size
      (2) color/finish
      (3) material
      (4) color application
      (5) quantity
   c. Header
      (1) size
      (2) color
   d. Header typography
      (1) style/size
      (2) color
      (3) position
      (4) application
      (5) message (include message schedule form)
      (6) letter/word/line spacing
   e. Directory inserts
      (1) size
      (2) type style/size
      (3) type color
      (4) background color
      (5) layout
      (6) message (include message schedule form)

  f. Mounting
  g. Tackboard
   (1) color
   (2) material
  h. Edge/fastener finish
3. Interior Signs
  a. Item Identification
  b. Panel
   (1) size
   (2) color
   (3) material
   (4) color application
   (5) quantity
  c. Typography
   (1) style
   (2) size
   (3) color
   (4) layout
   (5) message (include message schedule
    form)
   (6) application
   (7) letter/word/line spacing
  d. Edge finish

LETTER FORMS

Geometry can produce legible letters, but art
alone makes them beautiful. Art begins where
geometry ends, and imparts to letters a character
transcending mere measurement. —Paul Standard

Typography is a servant—the servant of thought
and language to which it gives visible existence.
        —T. M. Cleland

Although several early signage programs were
extensive enough to warrant design of totally new
alphabets or the modification of existing alphabets
(as in the case of the British Underground Rail and
London's Heathrow Airport systems, among
others), there is little need today for duplicating
such challenging design efforts.

  The typefaces illustrated here were selected as
the most suitable for signage systems. Other than
satisfying an underlying requirement for aesthetic
and suitability qualities, the only criteria a
typeface must meet are legibility and readability.
These two requirements in themselves narrow the
choices to a relative few.

  All letter faces differ in the way they are
constructed, in thickness, in contrast of strokes,
and in the proportion between stroke and counter.
This is generally referred to as height. They are also
supplied in varying shapes and proportions such as
extra condensed, condensed, standard, and
expanded.

  Most typefaces are available in several weights.
The character of the letters remains the same but
may be available in a range of weights, from light
to ultrabold.

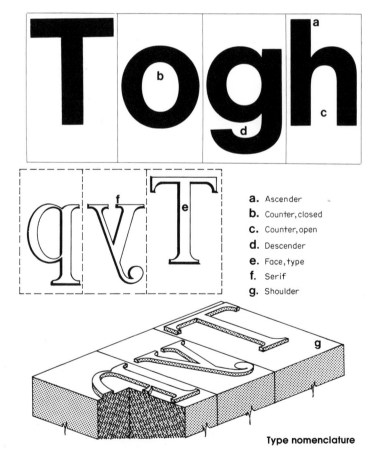

a. Ascender
b. Counter, closed
c. Counter, open
d. Descender
e. Face, type
f. Serif
g. Shoulder

Type nomenclature

Helvetica

ABCDEFGH
IJKLMNOP
QRSTUVW
XYZ &?!ß£$
abcdefghijkl
mnopqrstuv
wxyz 1234
567890(;)

Helvetica Medium

ABCDEFGHI
JKLMNOPQ
RSTUVWXY
Z&?!ß£$
abcdefghijkl
mnopqrstuv
wxyz12345
67890;

Univers 55

ABCDEFGHIJKL
MNOPQRSTUV
WXYZabcdefg
hijklmnopqrstuv
wxyz12345678
90&&?!ß£$(;)

Univers 65

ABCDEFGHIJK
LMNOPQRST
UVWXYZ abc
defghijklmnop
qrstuvwxyz12
34567890&&?
!ß£$(;)

Optima

ABCDEFGHIJKL
MNOPQRSTUV
WXYZ abcdefg
hijklmnopqrstu
vwxyz 1234567
890&?!£$ß(;)

Optima Semibold

ABCDEFGHIJK
LMNOPQRSTU
VWXYZabcdef
ghijklmnopqrst
uvwxyz123456
7890&?!£$ß()

Melior

ABCDEFGHIJK
LMNOPQRST
UVWXYZabc
defghijklmnopq
rstuvwxyz1234
567890&?!$;

Craw Clarendon

ABCDEFGH
IJKLMNOP
QRSTUVW
XYZ &?!ß£$
abcdefghijkl
mnopqrstuv
wxyz123456
7890 ()

The reason for providing alphabets in this variety of weights, of course, is to present the designer with alternatives for supplying emphasis or impact.

In selecting a typeface for signage, one of these few styles that have been specifically designed to meet the special requirements of signage should be used. The face should be simple in style and form so that proportions and shapes can be seen and easily recognized. The choice of weight is important because, in contrast to print, the eye has less time to absorb message content from a greater distance and must register and discern messages quickly in often distracting surroundings.

Unusual letter construction and unfamiliar proportions between strokes and counters are difficult to read and should be avoided.

The selection of a sans-serif alphabet for most signage applications would appear to be a natural choice. However, the disadvantage of using a serif typeface is not so much in legibility as it is in developing and applying a simple system for letter spacing and assembly. Serifs, in creating open counters, make the layout of words with correct interspacing more difficult to determine by mechanical means than between sans-serif letters.

Use of any single typeface for all applications is neither practical nor desirable. It is essential, therefore, that the typeface ultimately selected can be used consistently throughout the sign system.

The illustrations presented here are developed around Helvetica medium type and are intended only as examples of specific considerations that will apply generally to any typeface selected for signage application.

Letter/Word/Line Spacing

Of the many elements that combine to produce a successful sign system, none is more essential than design continuity. The graphic matrix upon which this is established is an array of evenly divisible and multiplicable square grid units that repeat the incremental proportions of the selected typeface. Once established, this grid permits the uniform establishment of the format of the letter, word, and line spacing for all message areas and sign panels comprising the system.

Other elements which contribute to design continuity, such as color, contrast, scale, and configuration, are also important and are discussed in this section.

When assembling letters for a sign panel, careful attention must be given to the positioning of all message elements, which are always controlled by module and grid. The letter, word, and line spacing recommendations illustrated on pages 34 and 35 are derived from the proportional relationships of traditional cold type.

Despite the fact that many of the point sizes used in printing do not readily convert to the linear scale used in signage, there are enough common sizes to permit limited interchange. However, because minute differences between the two systems of measurement exist and become visibly evident in sizes of type above 48 points, it is strongly recommended that this size be accepted as the maximum in the point scale to be used in message strip requirements of signage.

Type measurement in the point scale refers to the size of the "shoulder" on which the typeface is fixed, not the height of the typeface. In the case of Helvetica, this shoulder measurement corresponds to the 3 in the 2:3 ratio of the line spacing grid, or, as in the illustration shown, the 12 in the 8:12 ratio. A simple table of equivalent conversions would be:

Shoulder height of type-size designation		Actual type-face cap height		Typeface cap height in inches
9 points	=	6 points	=	$1/_{12}$ in
18 points	=	12 points	=	$1/_6$ in
48 points	=	36 points	=	$1/_2$ in
96 points	=	72 points	=	1 in

If the table were carried to the nearest equivalent of 2-in cap height, it should read:

192 points = 144 points = 2 in

However, this is not so. Actually, the conversion of this 192-point size of Helvetica measures $2^1/_{12}$ in or, instead of the actual letter cap height measuring 144 points (if the two measurement systems were precisely compatible), it measures 150 points.

Since most dry-transfer (rub-on) letters and photoprint type master templates, such as Headliner, Compu-Type, etc., were designed to produce copy intended for volume printing, use of the point scale of measurement for such is understood. So, until master templates producing type in the linear scale are made available, it is recommended that the print medium typefaces be used only for those elements of signage where economy and convenience dictate, and where compatibility with the signs' linear scaled lettering is established.

If, in order to support the environment in which it is intended to function, a signage system is determined to require a more precise and distinctive spacing grid, either the designer or the fabricator may be called upon to devise such as part of the contractual obligation.

In most cases, however, the use of the generally accepted sign industry terminology of "close, normal or standard, and open" letterspacing will be sufficient. Generally all signs, exterior and interior, should utilize "normal or standard" letterspacing. In any event, the system in this section is primarily intended for use as a tool to determine message line lengths arithmetically without actual detailing of individual sign layouts or mock-ups.

If a sign fabricator requests a change in spacing due to the length of a message, consideration of close or open spacing may be in order providing the fabricator first submits a sample for approval.

Although a maximum of 30 characters per line is recommended, this quantity may vary with different type styles.

Consistency of spacing between all message elements is essential to the development of a readable sign and is relatively easy to achieve. Usually, close letter and word spacing will be decreased by half the normal spacing, and open letter and word spacing will be increased by half the normal spacing. In any case, line spacing should not be affected. See pages 34–35.

Within the group of typefaces recommended for signage, the ratios of X-height to cap height range from Optima and Melior at approximately 2:3, to Univers and Helvetica at approximately 3:4. Whereas the 3:4 ratio supports the use of the X height as the basic unit of spacing control, the 2:3 ratio supports the use of the cap height as the basic unit most generally applicable to spacing control of all other typefaces. In the case of the 3:4 ratio both X height and cap height produce identical line spacing, and, except for an arbitrary division of the base units into a convenient scale of subunits for letter and word spacing controls, are interchangeable.

The system illustrated represents the minimum permissible spaces between lines of letters on sign faces. The designer should think in terms of selecting sign panels which are divisible into a number of equal-sized message units. A 48-in-high sign might consist of two 24-in units, three 16-in units, four 12-in units, six 8-in units, etc. Each unit consists of 12 (6- or 3-in) equal vertical divisions. The lettering for those units will ocupy two-thirds of the vertical height of the unit, or 8 (4- or 2-in) divisions. Thus, 1-in lettering will require a 1½-in unit, 2-in lettering will require a 3-in unit, 6-in lettering will require a 9-in unit, etc.

Eight (4- or 2-in) vertical divisions will always represent the cap height. Distance from the left edge of the sign panel to the beginning point of a lettering layout is generally equal to no less than the cap height of the sign's dominant message (including the frame if used). The message unit may become the edge of the sign itself or it may become part of a directional sign with space allowed for the insertion of an arrow, or when specified, a symbol.

This grid matrix also corresponds to the proportion prescribed by the International Organization for Standardization (ISO) for the design and submission for consideration and acceptance of graphic symbols (refer to p. 47).

Alphabet showing body-block proportions: A-Z ▶

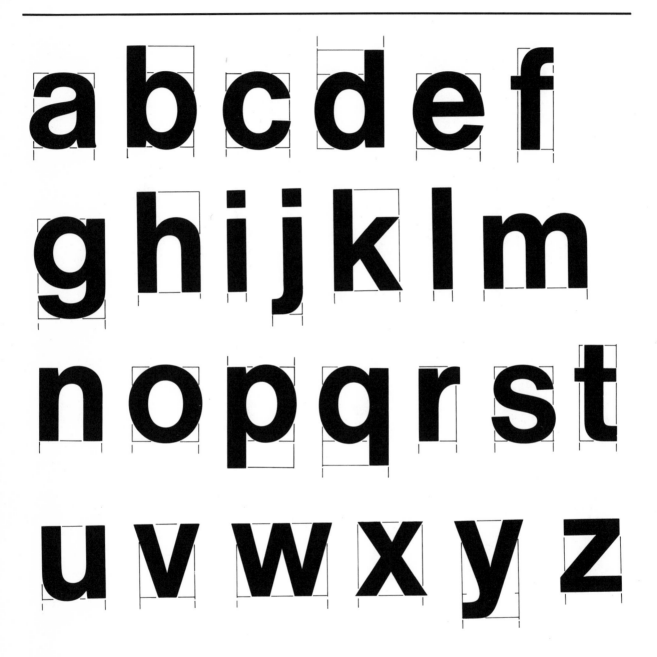

Alphabet showing body-block proportions: a-z

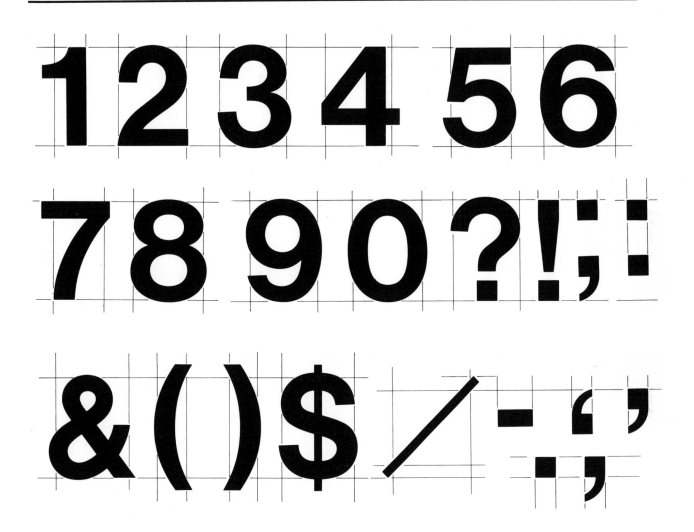

Numerals and punctuation

letter spacing

When positioning the first letter of a line of type in multiline flush-left messages, locate the left line of the body block on the margin. This will achieve perceptual vertical alignment of all first letters.

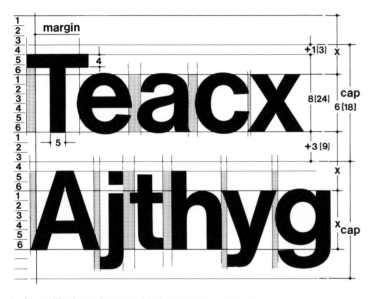

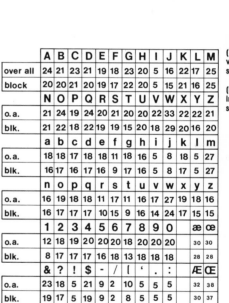

Typical subunit proportions

In positioning subsequent letters to form words of the sign's message or messages, use of the phantom rectangular body block lines in conjunction with unit spacing indicated to the right of this text should produce visually pleasing letter and word spacing as well as perceptual, not actual, level lateral alignment.

Note: These figures reflect spacing for interior signs based on the four subunit width of straight lateral or cross strokes. For exterior signs add one unit, based on the five-unit straight vertical strokes.

Unit indications (see right) have been rounded to the nearest whole number for convenience and are intended for use where visually close approximations are permissible.

(Left) Character widths in grid subunits

(Below) Letter spacing in grid subunits

	A	B	C	D	E	F	G	H	I	J	K	L	M
over all	24	21	23	21	19	18	23	20	5	16	22	17	25
block	20	20	21	20	19	17	22	20	5	15	21	16	25
	N	O	P	Q	R	S	T	U	V	W	X	Y	Z
o.a.	21	24	19	24	20	21	20	20	22	33	22	22	21
blk.	21	22	18	22	19	19	15	20	18	29	20	16	20
	a	b	c	d	e	f	g	h	i	j	k	l	m
o.a.	18	18	17	18	18	11	18	16	5	8	18	5	27
blk.	16	17	16	17	16	9	17	16	5	8	17	5	27
	n	o	p	q	r	s	t	u	v	w	x	y	z
o.a.	16	19	18	18	11	17	11	16	17	27	19	18	16
blk.	16	17	17	17	10	15	9	16	14	24	17	15	15
	1	2	3	4	5	6	7	8	9	0		æ	œ
o.a.	12	18	19	20	20	20	18	20	20	20		30	30
blk.	8	17	17	17	16	18	13	18	18	18		28	28
	&	?	!	$	-	/	[	'	.	:		Æ	Œ
o.a.	23	18	5	21	9	2	10	5	5	5		32	38
blk.	19	17	5	19	9	2	8	5	5	5		30	37

	vw y	j	x	z	ft	as goq	cde pru	mn kl	bhi	7	1	4	356 890	2
T	0	2	0	0	5	0	0	0	5	9	8	3	4	4
VWY	3	1	2	2	2	2	2	4		9	7	2	4	4
KX	0	0	4	4	2	2	2	3	4	5	5	2	2	4
AL	0	1	4	4	3	3	3	4	4	4	4	3	4	
F	2	0	2	3	3	2	3	3	4	6	7	4	4	3
Z	3	0	3	4	3	3	3	4	4	6	6	4	3	4
P	5	0	3	4	4	3	3	4	4	6	7	6	4	4
Q						5			6	7	6	5	4	
BCDORS	4	0	2	4	5	4	4	4	6	7	6	4	4	
EGHIJMNU	4	0	3	4	4	4	4	4	6	6	6	4	4	
ahmn	4	3	3	4	4	4	4	4						
kvwxy	4	1	3	4	3	2	2	4	4					
r	4	1	3	4	5	3	3	4	4					
ce æœ	3	0	0	3	4	4	4	4	4					
s	3	0	1	4	3	4	4	4	4					
bop	3	0	1	3	4	4	4	4	4					
dgijlqu	4	3	3	4	4	4	4	4	4					
ftz	4	0	2	4	4	3	3	4	4					

4	!	12
4	-	4
4	"	4
4	?	12
12	$	4
8	&	8
4	; :	12
4	]	12
12	[	4
4	/	4

	7	1	4	2356 890	,
7	6	6	2	4	0
1	4	5	5	5	6
4	4	5	5	5	6
2356890	5	5	5	5	4
· ,	0	4	6	4	4

(Opposite and above)
Typical letter/word/line spacing

Arrows

Research on arrow design tends to invalidate any attempt to determine a "best" arrow—or even a series of arrows that remain equally efficient under all conditions. Illumination and color combinations play a large role in the effectiveness of all arrow designs.

An attempt should be made, nevertheless, to pick a "standard" arrow and stay with it, as far as practical, throughout a given system. The selection of an appropriate arrow should be made on the basis of its compatibility with the selected typeface.

The arrow, like the alphabet, is keyed to a unit spacing (grid) system and will always be placed within a module square of its own on a sign panel. The arrow occupies the same fixed position in the grid pattern (square) and is installed to the left or to the right of the sign message as a complete square unit in accordance with the direction indicated.

Arrows may point in any one of eight directions: up (generally used for things that will be found straight ahead, but this can also indicate a floor above), down (generally used to indicate things to be found on a floor below), up left or right (generally used at the bottom of stairs or escalators), and down left or right (generally used at the heads of stairs or escalators).

Never use arrows pointing in "intermediate" directions between the directions shown.

The Panel System

The panel system outlined here is based upon three factors: the size of type used, space required for a line of type, and the length of the message (the number of letter characters per line of copy). It is important to understand that there is a fixed relationship between the letter size used and the sign panel size.

In discussing the panel system, the word "message" refers to the graphic or copy of a defined size, "message unit" refers to a vertical subdivision of a sign in which the defined message is positioned, and "message area" is the defined space for all messages within a sign panel. "Sign panel" is the total defined area of the sign. Throughout this system, reference will always be made to the sign panel exclusive of any type of frame, enclosure, or unique shape.

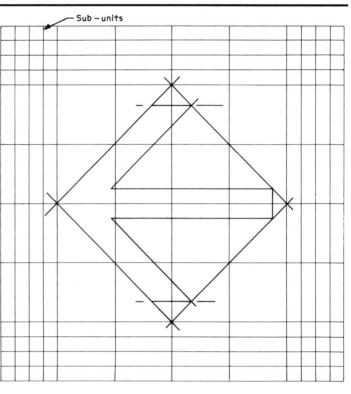

Sub–units

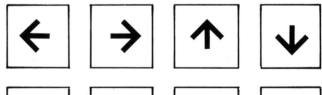

Approved arrow directions

Arrows and their orientation

Type Size

The first step in determining a sign panel size is to determine the size of the type to be used. As a general rule, for exterior vehicular and pedestrian signs, the use of 1-in cap height as a minimum for each 30 ft as a maximum viewing distance will provide minimum legibility.

At this point it may be helpful to repeat the explanation of the difference between legibility and readability. Legibility is the viewer's physical ability to see and distinguish a sign and its contained message. Readability is the viewer's ability to understand the message.

To account for angular distortion and varying imposed conditions on signs, use of 1-in cap height for each 30 ft of viewing distance is recommended for interior signs, and ¹/₂-in cap height is the minimum size recommended for all signs except in directories and maps, and for other special requirements.

The size of letter used will depend on the distance at which it is expected to be read within certain environmental and lighting conditions. Where a sign panel contains more than one size of type, the dominant message will generally control its location and placement orientation, because of the hierarchy of message importance.

It should be noted here that the Canadian system of viewing distances (50 ft per inch of letter height) is based on the X height, which appears at some variance with the cap-height formula. However, both are intended for use as guides, and final determinations of letter heights should be made only as a result of field testing. The following table of X-height viewing distances has been converted from the Canadian metric system to linear inches and feet.

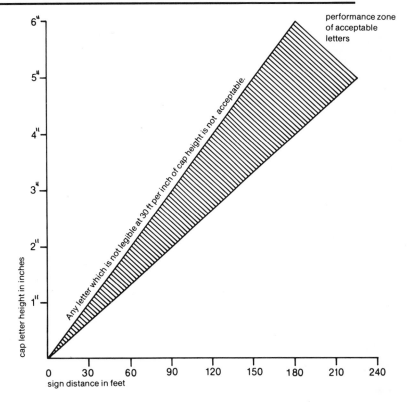

Cap-height viewing distances

Character X height, in	Reading distance, ft	Traffic speed, mph
0.20	10	Pedestrian
0.24	12	
0.32	16	
0.40	20	
0.48	24	
0.60	30	
0.80	40	
1.00	50	
1.20	60	
1.60	80	
		Vehicular
2.00	100	10–20
2.40	120	10–20
3.20	160	20–30
4.00	200	20–30
4.80	240	40–60
6.00	300	40–60
8.00	400	40–60

Message Unit

Once the type size has been determined for a given message, the message unit can be defined. By using a 2:3 ratio, it can be determined that a given size of type will require a certain vertical space. *Regardless of type sizes, this ratio will always apply, providing proportional continuity.* The following quick-reference table relates unit size to type size:

Cap height of type	=	Message unit
1/2 in	=	3/4 in
3/4 in	=	1 1/8 in
1 in	=	1 1/2 in
2 in	=	3 in
3 in	=	4 1/2 in
4 in	=	6 in
6 in	=	9 in

Message Length

For maximum ease of reading interior signs, any given line in a sign should not exceed 30 characters in width, including upper- and lower-case letters and spaces between words.

If a letter character of a word projects beyond the character limit per line, determine whether a second line could be used to complete the message or if the panel could be extended by a 3-in increment of width (or multiples of 3-in increment) to contain the message on one line. If neither is practical and the message is being applied to the sign panel by the photo silk-screen process, the entire message unit may be photographically reduced to fit within the established limit of the message area. In this case the perceivable difference of such proportional reduction should be negligible.

It is important to understand that the type of message will dictate the vertical or horizontal format of a sign. Whether for exterior or interior signs, always be sure that the size selected can be accommodated by the site selected for its installation.

To assist in quickly determining the approximate sign panel size the following table reflects various panel widths required for given type sizes allowing for a maximum of 30 characters per line:

Type size, in	panel width, in
1/2	12
3/4	18
1	21
1 1/2	30
2	45

The sizes are based on Helvetica Medium typeface with normal letter spacing.

Regarding exterior signs, it may take a motorist as much as half a second to read and react to a line of message on a sign. In order to avoid creating safety hazards, no sign for motorists should, in principle, exceed 16 words or 4 lines, or take more than 3 or 4 seconds for the motorist to read and react. Signs for pedestrians' use may, within reason, be any length up to the recommended limit of 30 characters per line.

The Sign Panel

The actual panel size of a sign will be determined by the type size, message length, and message unit as previously discussed. There are, however, minimums recommended concerning panel size. No sign panel should be smaller than 3 x 6 in with a maximum provision for four lines of 1/2 in (cap height) of copy.

Any limit to the maximum size of a sign panel will depend largely upon the limitations imposed by the materials' manufacturer, the fabricator, and/or costs.

The shape of sign panels will vary from square to rectangle and from vertical to horizontal in format. Combinations of formats may occur within a single sign may consist of a 3- x 12-in horizontal number panel and a 3- x 12-in message panel with four message lines, both panels stacked to form a 6- x 12-in sign panel. This size is exclusive of any frame. A second example is a 6-in-square symbol panel located to the side of a 6- x 12-in message panel forming a 6- x 18-in overall sign panel.

The message area determination will always be the same regardless of the ultimate shape of the overall sign.

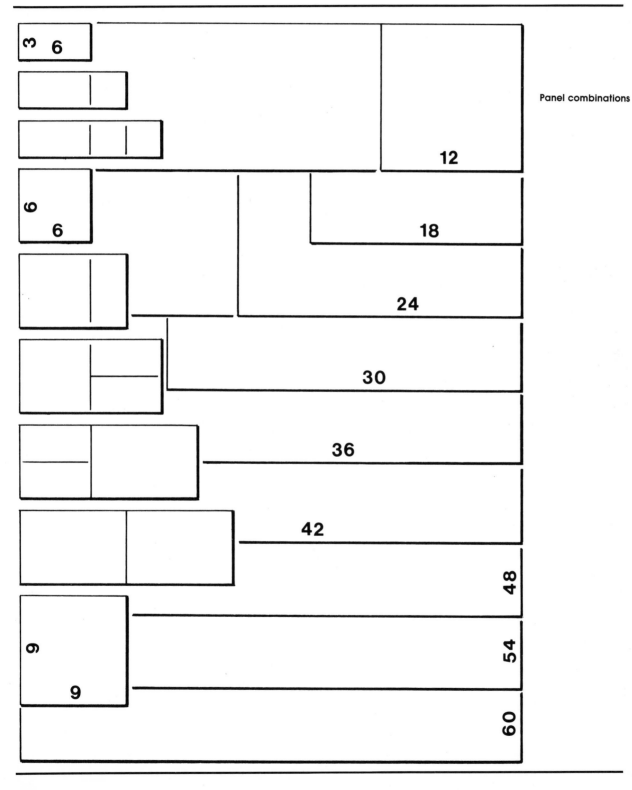

Panel combinations

Layout

Layout is descriptive of graphic design that, like plain language, has more to do with readability than legibility. Layout is what the lay person calls the "setup" and concerns the spatial relationships between or among all of the components.

As styles and fashions change, so do ideas about layout, and it is quite impossible to be dogmatic about "standards" (which do not really exist anyway) on any of these subjects. The only thing that can be required is that a style, once established in a signage system (as, for example, the arrangement of copy), be consistently followed in all of the components that make up the system.

The matter of flush left, centered, or flush right has been the subject of continuing debate in the design community but is chiefly an aesthetic consideration. Centering applies mainly to lines that are composed entirely in caps. When lines are composed in upper- and lowercase letters, the centered line can look very untidy. This is particularly true when there is a large discrepancy in the length of lines, or when there is an unfortunate visual interaction between the descenders of one line and the ascenders of the next.

Copy arrangements

**The quick
brown fox jumped**

**The quick
brown fox jumped**

The flush-left arrangement is highly recommended, and flush-right arrangement should be adopted only in certain directional signs because it is always better, from the reader's point of view, to bring the eye back to the same relative position at the beginning of each line.

Consideration should be given to the efficiency of the message by placing left-pointing arrows flush left on the sign (as well as the message that relates to them) and by placing right-pointing arrows flush right on the sign (along with their respective messages). By the same token, arrows pointing straight ahead should be placed left or right on the sign, depending upon the location of the sign relative to traffic flow.

Although there are some notable exceptions in use today, it is accepted that in terms of readability, *messages in upper- and lowercase are some 10 to 12 percent more readable than those set in caps only.*

A word set in upper- and lowercase has a more familiar "word shape" than the same word set in caps.

The same word set in upper- and lowercase occupies 30 to 35 percent less space than when set in caps.

Uppercase, on the other hand, because it forms messages that are conveniently regular in shape, is easier to handle from the viewpoint of layout.

Word shapes in all caps and upper- and lowercase letters

word "shapes"

Changeability

Most sign systems should focus on ease of changeability. Signs requiring change on a periodic basis should be changeable by any authorized individual and should not produce excessive wasted or nonreusable parts. Minimal production or machine work should be required. The changeable elements should be vandalproof and unexposed to removal by unauthorized personnel. Specific priorities must be established for varying degrees of change of frequency, and signs should be developed accordingly. Ideally, changes should be accomplished with in-house personnel.

For the most part, changeability is important in the following areas:

- Location

- Mounting

- Room function

- Office identification

- Directory listing

Building and floor directories and area/office identification signs must be designed to allow change of individual messages. Message strips must be interchangeable from one floor directory or room identification sign to another within a specific facility.

Room Numbering System

Due to the wide range of sizes, shapes, types, and interior configurations of built environments, a standard room numbering system has not been developed. Room numbering must be tailored to each requirement.

Note: Because so little definitive knowledge of the interrelationships of color, lighting, and considerations regarding the handicapped is presently available, only the most generally applicable recommendations are made here.

Color/Color Coding

In choosing color for sign panel background and graphics, discretion should be used in determining compatibility with the environment in which the sign is to be placed. Available light, whether ambient or artificial, will be an important factor in determining sign colors.

Color coding may be used if desired, but is not addressed here. There are certain basic controls, however, which should be mentioned as guidelines for establishing a color-coded system.

The mind has an extremely limited memory for colors and, when they are utilized for the purposes of color coding, no more than five or six should be used. Beyond this number the memory becomes overtaxed and cannot make proper associations.

A color such as turquoise tends to be called different names by different people, some referring to it as blue, others calling it green. This leads to ambiguity and confusion. Therefore, colors selected for color coding should be those that are always referred to by a universal name. There are certain colors which exist in a wide variety of shades and tints while still retaining a nameable quality.

All colors selected for a color code should be selected on the assumption that they will be seen under conditions of artificial illumination as well as in daylight. It is therefore essential that they be tested under actual lighting conditions.

Some colors (primaries) already have strong connotations or meanings and should, therefore, never be used in any other context. Colors that are available for color coding should be used in a consistent manner within the system established.

It is essential when color coding is used that it be expressed systematically throughout the color-coded areas, and not limited to maps only.

For purposes of ascertaining the brightness differential of any given combination of two colors, it is immaterial which is used for the background and which for the message. They may, in fact, be interchanged within the system.

The main objective is to arrive at a brightness differential of at least 75 percent using universally named colors. By lighting any of these colors the brightness is, of course, increased accordingly. So long as the color remains recognizable under

these conditions it may be used, regardless of how much it departs from the midrange.

The formula used in calculating brightness differential is as follows:

$$\frac{B1 - B2}{B1} \times 100 = \text{reflectance (percent)}$$

*B*1 stands for the percentage of reflectance of the brighter of the two, and *B*2 for the darker of the two colors. (These values are available from paint manufacturers.)

It is recommended that color systems such as Pantone matching system, Munsel color system, and Container Coordination color harmony system be used as a color-matching reference.

Signs for the Handicapped

This is (and is likely to continue to be) a much-debated and highly controversial area of the signage requirement. Since a single cost-effective solution cannot equally serve in all cases, only minimal recommendations believed to be common to all considerations are noted.

Federally owned or federally supported installations and facilities must conform, and privately owned or privately funded installations and facilities should voluntarily conform to Federal Propery Management Regulation, Amendment D-22, Section 101-17.703, which adopts "American Standards Specifications for making buildings and facilities accessible to or usable by the handicapped, No. A117.1-1961." These standards require raised letters and/or numbers to identify rooms or offices (Section 5-11, for the visually handicapped).

In all cases specific considerations for all handicapped should be given in the following areas:

- Designated building entrance access

- Designated parking areas

- Direction to and identification of accessible convenience facilities (rest rooms)

- Directional signs

- Room identification

Additional consideration for the visually handicapped should be provided within elevator cabs. This is the responsibility of facility A/E (architect/engineer) or manager in coordination with the elevator manufacturer or manufacturers.

In all applications of raised messages, the character should be raised in height $^{1}/_{32}$ in to $^{3}/_{64}$ in.

All regulatory symbols used in interior applications should include raised word descriptions in addition to the symbol.

Governmental Agency Seals and
Corporate Identity Logotypes

The use of government agency seals and corporate identity logotypes on exterior building identification should be discouraged. However, certain situations may favor the use of a seal or logotype with building identification.

Any identifying seal may be used inside buildings for area or office identification. Generally such seals will be incorporated into the primary identification sign.

Situations may arise which call for a large seal. These will generally be of a cutout or cast nature without a controlled background. The material from which these may be produced should be selected to meet both performance and cost considerations.

A decision to leave existing government seals in place or to use them with building identification shall be made by the regional authority.

The use of corporate seals and logotypes on/or in private facilities will be determined on a case basis.

In existing buildings where a new sign system is to be installed, there will often be certain exterior or interior sign devices of a permanent nature, such as relief or incised letters in masonry walls, freestanding or wall-recessed items which, if removed, would result in unsightly openings or other undesirable consequences. It is understandable if these are not removed, but this is a decision to be made jointly by management and the designer.

Illumination

All signs for exterior and interior use should utilize available ambient light from existing light sources where it is considered sufficient. No internal illumination is suggested, except for building directories. Internal illumination is required for exit signs.

If exterior signs are determined to require lighting, flood lighting directed from the ground level may be provided. Internal illumination should be considered only if necessary.

Reflectorized lettering may be used for vehicular signs.

Stock, readily available and Underwriters Laboratory (UL)-approved, should be used for all illuminated signs.

Sign function is all-important; consequently, for all regulatory or warning signs (whether exterior or interior), where fidelity of color and message are essential, sufficient illumination level and color balance must be provided, even if these entail use of additional light fixtures.

Studies conducted by experimental psychologist Dr. Robert Glass at the National Bureau of Standards (NBS) on different pigment compositions under various energy-efficient light sources discovered that most common red paints under low-pressure sodium lamps appear gray, under high-pressure sodium lamps they appear orange, while under an uncoated mercury light source they appear brown. However, a fluorescent red appears red under all light sources tested. This occurs because fluorescent colors absorb light at a different rate than when emitting it, thus causing each to be visually perceived as a true color.

Based on these findings, the NBS group made recommendations to the Occupational Safety and Health Administration (OSHA) which will ensure that the appropriate safety colors remain perceptually true under different light sources.

As a guide in determining acceptable levels of illumination, signs should receive the same amount of foot-candles of illumination as is considered acceptable for office working areas.

Although studies will continue to produce a number of new energy-efficient light sources, there are only four basic types of illumination presently recommended for signs: incandescent, fluorescent, high-intensity discharge, and reflective.

Incandescent illumination is produced by a common incandescent bulb or quartz-iodine lamp. Both light small areas with high intensity, but their light output is low and not energy-efficient. Their color rendition emphasizes reds and yellows.

Fluorescent illumination uses common fluorescent tubes in a wide range of colors. They light large areas with low intensity, their light output is fair to good, and their color rendition varies according to the color of the tube.

High-density discharge illumination uses mercury vapor lamps in cool to warm colors. Light is produced by an electric arc in mercury vapor. They light small areas with very high intensity, their light output is high, and their color rendition is only fair, producing bluish and greenish casts on normal tones.

Reflective illumination depends upon an independent, exterior light source controlled by the user and not the designer.

Signs with an interior light source should be adequately sealed against weather and insects which will be attracted to the lighting units. All electrical components should be UL-approved, and the rating of each component checked to ensure that each is designed to handle the required lighting wattage. Lighting units that develop high temperatures must be adequately ventilated and spaced from materials that can be damaged by heat.

If the light source is excessively bright, "irradiation" or "halation" will cause the individual letters (if they are translucent against an opaque background) to merge with their neighbors, and the message will become blurred and ineffective. If the letters are opaque against a translucent background, halation will cause them to appear inconsistent in thickness and virtually disappear or lose much of their legibility. A white letter on a black background is more legible than any other arrangement due to an optical illusion known as the "ona" effect, which causes a white letter to appear larger (or advance) to the viewer. The degree of this effect is directly related to letter spacing.

An exterior light source provides the simplest and least expensive way to light a sign, in terms of both installation and maintenance.

Ambient light, or spill from existing light sources, may offer sufficient illumination to make a sign readable. If so, there will be no need to provide additional lighting, thus reducing the initial and long-term costs of the sign system considerably. Designers planning to rely on this method for illuminating their signs should carefully study the effects of color contrast.

CHAPTER SIX

Design Guidelines for Symbols and Symbol-Signs

A symbol becomes more meaningful and evokes human responses when, and only when, a perceiver of that symbol projects meaning into it and responds to it in terms of the meaning which he has learned as appropriate for that symbol.
—Lawrence K. Frank

This section is unique in that it deals with "symbols" as a distinct and separate graphic device within the overall signage system, and may, as a consequence, necessitate exceptions to the parameters established in the design process for that system.

When their use is indicated, symbol-signs are more effective than lettered or typographic signs alone.

Evidence produced from scientific testing clearly indicates that symbol-signs combining distinctive colors and shapes with graphic symbols are superior to those signs which employ monochromatic symbols in a single (usually square) shape.

Symbol-signs are intended to do more than identify objects. Symbol-signs also are used to regulate behavior (by telling us what we must not do or, alternatively, what we must do, and to warn us of potential or definite hazard); in addition, they identify things that have to do with public safety, emergency, and protection.

A symbol needs to express an idea in either of two ways: prohibition or obligation.

It is obvious that both of these cannot be expressed with the same graphic symbol; therefore, it is necessary to rely upon other elements to do this.

All of the functions that are demanded of symbol-signs (regulation, warning, and information) will be more effectively communicated through the systematic use of distinctive shapes and colors combined with graphic symbols.

No intention is made to affect, supersede, or replace signs or symbols for which nationally recognized standards have been developed and promulgated, such as those incorporated into the *Manual on Uniform Traffic Control Devices* issued by the U.S. Department of Transportation (DOT) Federal Highway Administration, and *Symbol Signs* (1974) and *Symbol signs 2* (1979), which are passenger/pedestrian-oriented symbols for use in transportation-related facilities. These publications were researched and prepared by the American Institute of Graphic Arts (AIGA) for the Office of Facilitation, Environment Safety, and Consumer Affairs, U.S. Department of Transportation.

Although the DOT documents are intended for use in transportation-related applications, it is strongly recommended that these documents also be utilized in determining the design, legends, placement, etc. of signs and symbols regulating all pedestrian and vehicular traffic.

Our purpose here is twofold:

1. To illustrate and explain the color/shape system, and to describe requirements for the design of symbol-signs to make recommendations for their use in circumstances where such symbol-signs are clearly applicable.

2. To establish the basis for ongoing discussions and development of symbols by those designers who manifest interest in or actually make extensive use of symbol-signs.

Types and Shapes of Symbol-Signs

The first graphic element we can rely on to express function categorically is shape. There are three basic and truly distinctive geometric plane shapes: circles, triangles, and squares (or rectangles).

There are three basic functions for which symbol-signs may be employed: regulation, warning, and information. Each type is represented by a graphic shape: *The circle is used for regulatory signs, the equilateral triangle is used for warning signs, and the square is used for information signs.*

Geometric shapes
for symbols

Classification of Symbol-Signs

Each of the three basic symbol-sign shapes (regulation, warning, and information) is divided into two classifications, which are shown here with further details about their color and design characteristics.

The three types
combined

Type 1: Regulation

Classification 1.1: Prohibition: All symbols in this classification denote an order for the prevention of an action (e.g., "No Smoking").

Prohibition symbols shall have a black symbol located inside a white field circumscribed by a red ring, diagonally bisected at 45° (315° to 135°) by a red slash. *Note:* The red slash is interrupted for the black symbol.

Classification 1.2: Obligation: All symbols in this classification denote an order for obligatory action (e.g., "Head Protection Must Be Worn!").

Obligatory symbols shall have a white symbol located inside a black disk.

Type 2: Warning

Classification 2.1: Caution: All symbols in this classification denote the presence of a potential hazard (e.g., "Men at Work").

Caution symbols shall have a black symbol located inside a solid yellow equilateral triangle.

Classification 2.2: Danger: All symbols in this classification denote the presence of a definite hazard (e.g., "Danger: Explosives").

Danger symbols shall have a white symbol inside a solid red equilateral triangle.

Type 3: Information

Classification 3.1: First Aid, Emergency, and Fire Protection: All symbols in this classification denote first-aid-related equipment as well as fire-protection and emergency equipment (e.g., "First-Aid Station," or "Fire Extinguisher").

First-aid and fire-protection symbol-signs shall have a white symbol located inside a green square or rectangle.

Classification 3.2: Miscellaneous: All symbols in this classification denote information not covered by any other classification (e.g., "Cafeteria").

Miscellaneous symbol-signs shall have a white symbol located inside a blue square or rectangle.

When, for aesthetic reasons only, it is deemed undesirable to have these miscellaneous symbol-signs in blue, they may be produced in any "neutral" color, providing:

1. The symbol is reversed (in a lighter color) from the "neutral" background.

2. The neutral background shall have a tonal value (on the gray scale) of not more than 60 percent and not less than 40 percent.

This exception applies exclusively to signs in this classification. There is no similar exception to signs in the other classifications.

Note: The grid matrix for symbol development prescribed by the ISO utilizes the metric scale. However, the 6 × 6 basic unit square may be constructed to any convenient scale because proportions thus established will remain constant and are consequently readily convertible to any other scale.

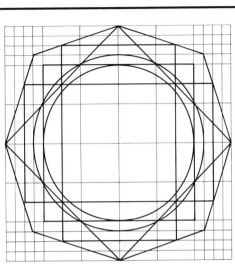

ISO grid matrix

Proportions of Symbol-Sign Shapes

As in the case of letter forms, optical adjustments must be made if all three shapes are to have a consistent "look" to them; i.e., it is desirable that the circle, the triangle, and the square, when viewed together, should appear to have the same height and a similarity of overall area.

Whatever scale is employed, the base of the triangle, the diameter of the circle, and the height/width of the square shall have the following relationship.

Note: The triangle and square are shown here in strict geometric form. In practice, these shapes will have rounded corners.

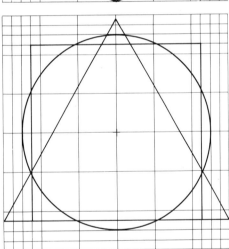

Size relationship
of geometric shapes

Border and Symbol Area of Symbol-Sign Shapes

The entire symbol-sign is either circular, triangular, or square. It is not just these shapes overlayed on a series of squares. In each case, a border is located inside the overall shape, giving definition to the color field inside it. And within this color field there is a definite area in which the symbol may be located.

All symbol-signs shall be surrounded by a white border. The width of the border on all shapes is 1/4 unit.

The maximum area that the symbol may occupy in each of the shapes is indicated by the broken line. It is located 1/4 unit from the inner edge of the respective borders.

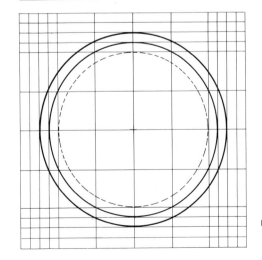

Border symbol areas

Corner Radii

Up to this point, the triangle and square have been shown with sharp (unrounded) corners. This is impractical from the point of view of potential vandalism and normal wear and tear. However, excessive rounding of the corners would render them as "intermediate figures"—which means that they would lose some or most of their inherent distinctiveness as shapes. For this reason, a nominal 5:1 ratio of outside radius (o/r) to inside radius (i/r) has been selected for all subsequent illustrations of symbol-signs (see right, below).

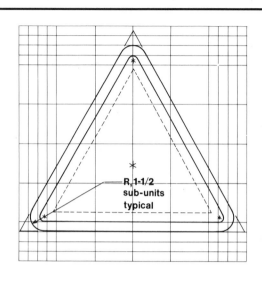

R,1-1/2
sub-units
typical

(Left and below)
Border symbol areas

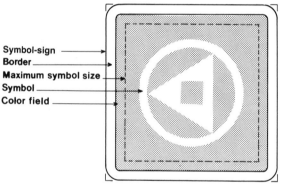

Symbol-sign
Border
Maximum symbol size
Symbol
Color field

Symbol-Sign Elements

The symbol-sign consists of several elements in addition to the characteristics described thus far.

Symbols

The graphic symbol should occupy not more than 50 percent of the color field in which it is located. The ideal proportion of symbol-size to color field will depend to some extent upon the 50 percent-maximum rule as well as the subjective aesthetic considerations of the designer.

When a new graphic symbol is developed the designer should strive toward a basic simplification of representational art and resist all temptation toward abstraction.

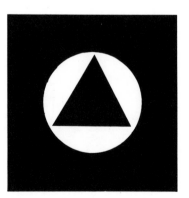

Color field/symbol proportions

Color

Just as each symbol-sign has its distinctive shape, each also has a distinctive color background. Thus shape and color are combined to reinforce communication effectively.

- Red for   Prohibition (1.1)
                          Danger (2.2)
- Green for   Emergency, first aid, fire protection (3.1)
- Yellow for   Caution (2.1)
- Blue for   Miscellaneous (3.2)
- Black for   Obligation (1.2)
- White

Note: Black is used for symbols in classifications 1.1 and 2.1. White is used for symbols in all other classifications. These colors may be identified by reference to the color tolerance charts available from the Office of Hazardous Materials, U.S. Department of Transportation, Washington, D.C.

1.1

2.2

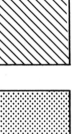

3.1

2.1

3.2

1.2

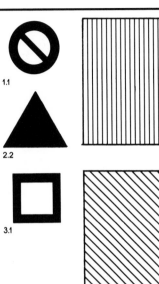

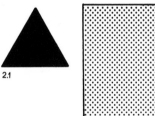

Color functions

Typical Symbol-Signs

The symbols shown here are not intended to
represent a "standard." Nor does their printing
herein constitute or imply an endorsement by any
"official" body. Some belong to a series of
copyrighted designs. Others are from the system
prepared by the AIGA for the DOT and are used
here solely to illustrate typical symbol-signs in the
various classifications.

Prohibition
1. No Smoking!
2. No Parking!
3. No Automobiles!

Obligatory
1. Eye Protection Must Be Worn!
2. Head Protection Must Be Worn!
3. Seat Belts Must Be Worn!
4. Foot Protection Must Be Worn!

Warning
1. Be Alert!
2. Men at Work
3. Electrical Hazard
4. Explosion Hazard

First Aid, Emergency, and Fire Protection
1. First Aid
2. Eyewash
3. Fire Extinguisher
4. Fire Hose

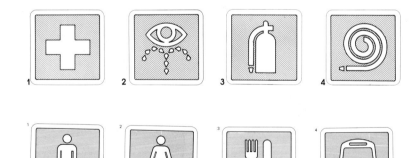

Miscellaneous
1. Men
2. Women
3. Cafeteria
4. Bus Stop

Legends

Symbols and symbol-signs frequently communicate
adequately on their own; however, just as
frequently it will be desirable to combine them with
words.

There are acceptable ways in which words—or legends—may be integrated into symbol-signs. In such cases local decisions must be made as to whether the "symbol" or the "type" will dictate the ultimate size of the symbol-sign plaque.

The decision, either way, may also indicate an exception to the general constraints implicit in the primary symbol-sign system concept.

Inasmuch as the symbol-sign shapes make no provision for accommodating legends, such provision—when legends are required—must be made in either one of two alternative ways shown here.

A. A rectangular blank of predetermined proportion on which are applied the legend and the symbol-sign

B. A plaque of predetermined proportion which displays the legend only and is fixed adjacent to and beneath the symbol

In A: the application of the symbol-sign to an oversized "blank" of such proportion as to accommodate the legend. Two variations of different proportions may be used depending on the length or size of the legend:

A.1 is proportioned (width to length) 6:9.

A.2 is proportioned (width to length) 6:12.

Note: Where the background of blank is white, there is no need for a separate white border around the symbol. This function is provided by the blank itself. The color field of the symbol-sign must not, however, be enlarged to cover that area which would normally be occupied by the border. Where the background of the blank is light gray, dark gray, or black, the white border must surround the color field.

In B: the addition of a small separate "plaque" located directly below the symbol-sign to which the legend may be applied. Two variations of different proportion may be used, depending on the length or size of the legend:

B.1 is proportioned (width to length) $4\frac{1}{2}:2\frac{1}{4}$.

B.2 is proportioned (width to length) $4\frac{1}{2}:4\frac{1}{2}$.

Note: The areas of these small message plaques are subdivided into half units and so become $4\frac{1}{2}:9$ and 9:9 units, i.e., equal to half and all of the square symbol area, respectively.

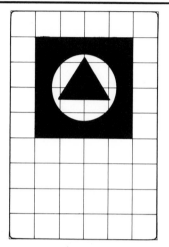
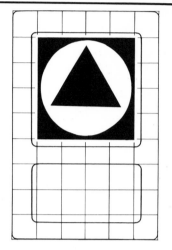
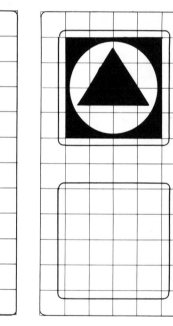

Alternate A—blank (combining)   **Alternate B—plaque (separate)**

Letter Styles and Letter Sizes for Legends: The letter style used for all legends should be the same as the one chosen for the basic symbol-sign system; upper- and lowercase, set flush left. The color of the legend should be as follows: (1) black legend on a white or light gray background or (2) white legend on a black or dark gray background.

There are three sizes of lettering that are recommended for legends. The unit size is based on the cap height. The size used in any application will be determined by the message length.

All three unit sizes are related to the half- (or 12-) unit grid and are as follows: (1) 1 unit, (2) 2 units, and (3) 3 units (for letter-size relationships only).

Typical legend letter size applications to blanks and plaques

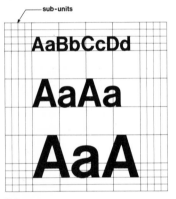

Unit sizes of type

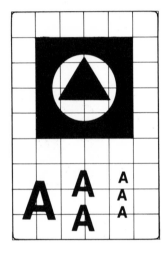

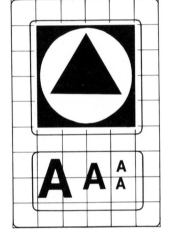

Legends are used only where local experience or other considerations validate the need for them. They are optional. However, if used, they should be as concise and simple as comprehension of meaning will permit. In all cases where symbol-signs must conform to Architectural and Transportation Barriers Compliance Board Requirements, raised-letter legends must be used.

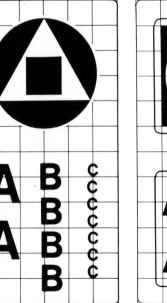

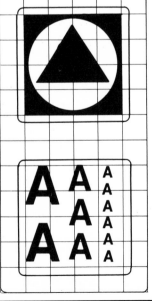

Note: All blanks and plaques shall have rounded corners which correspond to the corner radii of the symbol-signs. For layout purposes, a grid is shown superimposed on the blank and plaque. The size of this grid, based on the width of the blanks and plaques (which is constant), is 12 half-units for the large (combined) plaque and is 9 half-units for the small (separate) plaque. The grid will assist in determining the size of the lettering as well as the positioning of symbol-sign and legend on a blank or plaque. The 3:2 interline grid should be substituted for the blank/plaque proportional grid once the message area has been determined.

Note: Legends are generally set flush left, ragged right; however, when a one-word legend such as "Bus" or "Taxi" is used, it is appropriate to center the word visually on the sign.

In certain instances it will be necessary to use two type sizes within a single legend. This is done by using the grid, making sure that the appropriate interline spacing is maintained. As a general rule the interline spacing between two different sizes of letters should be equal to or greater than that required by the larger letter form.

Typical symbol applications
to blanks and plaques

**Applications of Multiple Symbols to
Blanks**

When symbol-signs are used in multiples on
directional signs, the sign area is determined by
using multiples of a type-A blank which will
accommodate two or more symbols, descriptive
legends, and/or directional arrows. The size of
type used for legends will be determined by the
length of the message.

More than one size of type should not be used
within any one sign or system (series) of signs.
Where two directions are indicated on a sign, a
blank space equal to one symbol width should be
maintained between symbols or groups of symbols.
No more than two directions should be displayed
on a given blank. In circumstances where more
than two directions are to be indicated, use
separate blanks.

Only after a review of the symbols contained in
available sources fails to find one to satisfy a
specific need should the effort to design a "new"
symbol be considered. (See the material on
sources in Part 4.)

It should be understood that preparatory to such
an effort most objects can be reduced to a
simple, readily recognized graphic representation
or symbol. By the same token, some familiar
services are similarly portrayable. On the other
hand, functions, especially those performed in a
related sequence of actions, range from difficult
to impossible in terms of depiction by intelligible
graphic symbols. Further, from an analysis of those
graphic symbols that have become widely used if
not "standard," a common elemental pattern
emerges to which all subsequent symbol design
efforts should conform, i.e.:

1. Begin by establishing the symbol's "referent"—
a unique brief description, rarely more than two
words.

2. Follow this with a graphic content description,
also unique, that amplifies the referent by clearly
identifying every graphic element comprising the
symbol as a whole.

3. These two steps combine to allow for more
than one configuration of the basic graphic
image, each being equally recognizable, while
reflecting the dominant local or native "styling."

4. Follow the graphic content description with
one or more brief optional legends applicable to
a given classification, i.e., (a) regulation, (b)
warning, and (c) information (to be used where
considered necessary).

Note: There is only one single referent for any
given symbol subject. Thus, "Smoking" (permitted)
and "No Smoking" will both fall under the same
referent entry (smoking).

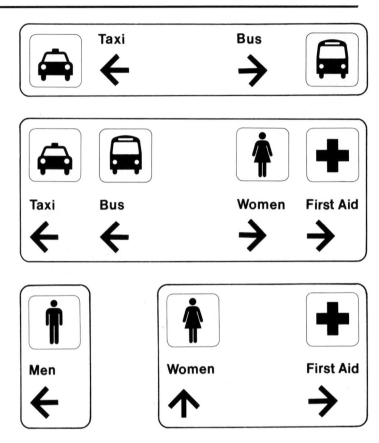

Applying multiple symbols to blanks

Even though this material has been primarily
directed to new symbols and new symbol-sign
concepts, it is quite possible that many existing
symbols' graphic content may be subtly modified,
strengthened, and/or enhanced by combining
them with a "classification shape" more conducive
to their intrinsic meaning which, as a
consequence, could also be a step toward
logical standardization.

Pages 55 through 63 exemplify design for symbol
and pictograph applications.

Design Guidelines for
Symbols and Symbol-Signs

New York City Health and Hospitals Corporation

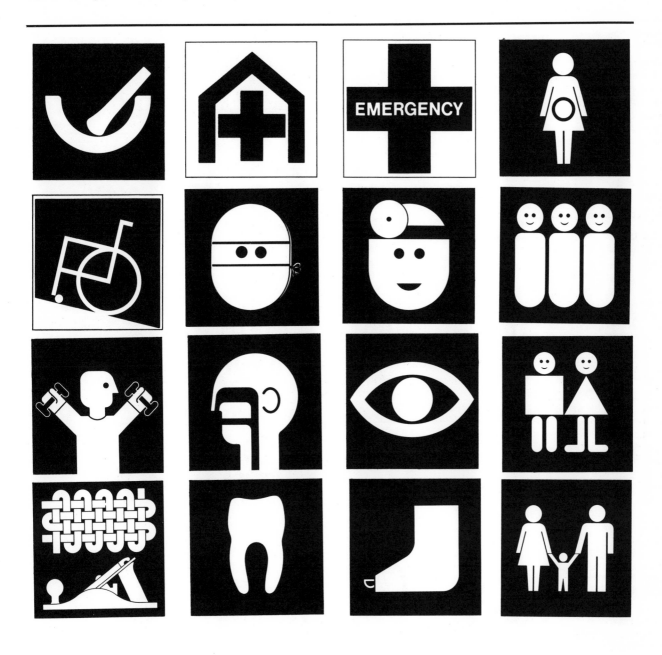

EMERGENCY

DOT transportation related symbols, combined system

**The Systems Concept
and How to Use It**

Mexico Olympics, 1968

Designed by Lance Wyman and Eduardo Terrazas of the
organizing committee's department of design, together
with a group of students from the industrial design department
of Ibero-American University, under the direction of
Professor Manual Villazon

**Design Guidelines for
Symbols and Symbol-Signs**

Washington Mall

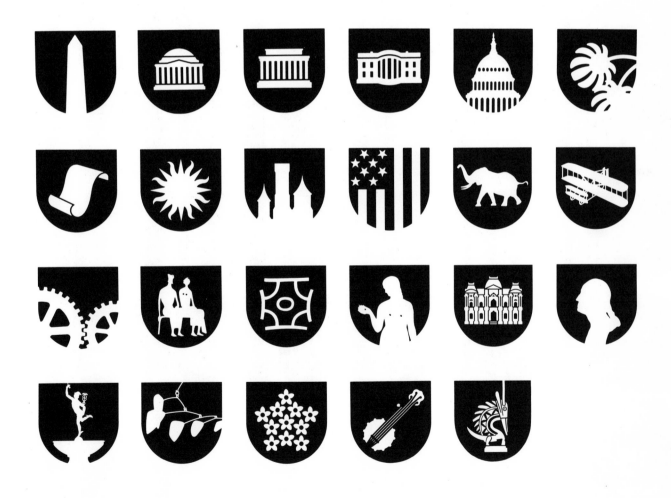

Client: Smithsonian Institution, Washington
Design firm: Wyman Synd Cannan Company
Designers: Lance Wyman, Bill Cannan
Design directors: Brian Flahive, Tucker Veimeister,
   Tom De Monse, Francisco Gallardo; assistant designers
   and production staff

National Zoo, Washington, D.C.

BEAR · BISON · BLESBOK · CAPE BUFFALO · CHEETAH · CRANE

CROCODILE · CROWNED CRANE · DEER · DUCK · EAGLE · ELEPHANT

FLAMINGO · GAZELLE · GIRAFFE · GNU · GOOSE · GORILLA

HIPPOPOTAMUS · JAGUAR · KIWI · KUDU · LION · LYNX

MONKEY · PANDA · PARROT · POLAR BEAR · RHINOCEROS · SEA LION

SEA OTTER · SNAKE · SWAN · TIGER · WOLF · WOOD DUCK

ZEBRA

Design firm: Wyman and Cannan Company, New York
Designers: Lance Wyman and Bill Cannan
Directors: Brian Flahive, Tucker Viemeister, Tom De Monse

Minnesota Zoo

Design firm: Lance Wyman Ltd.
Designers: Lance Wyman, design director; Stephen Schlott,
  assistant designer; Linda Iskander, coordination

Picto'grafics by Paul Arthur/VisuCom, Ltd.

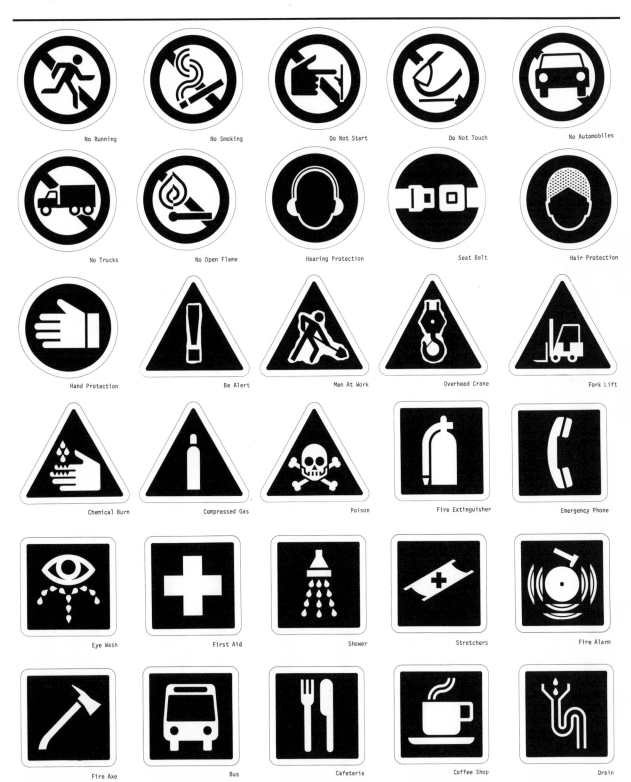

No Running	No Smoking	Do Not Start	Do Not Touch	No Automobiles
No Trucks	No Open Flame	Hearing Protection	Seat Belt	Hair Protection
Hand Protection	Be Alert	Men At Work	Overhead Crane	Fork Lift
Chemical Burn	Compressed Gas	Poison	Fire Extinguisher	Emergency Phone
Eye Wash	First Aid	Shower	Stretchers	Fire Alarm
Fire Axe	Bus	Cafeteria	Coffee Shop	Drain

CHAPTER SEVEN

Catalog of Signs

Few architects would give themselves the task of designing the sculpture or the murals for a building. They would be wise to receive help where graphic problems are involved.　　　　—Don Page

The catalog of signs provides a range of sign types which should generally satisfy most facility signage needs. The individual items within the catalog of signs will illustrate the physical sign type in elevation appearance with a typical message layout. In addition, cross-reference information is provided for design intent drawings and specifications for each sign type, located in their corresponding sections.

If a particular situation arises in which the catalog does not satisfy a need, follow the recommendations in Chapter 5, "The Next Step: Components of the System."

FACILITY IDENTIFICATION

Location

Any facility or building accessible to the public should be identified by a freestanding sign (preferred), or a sign applied to the facade of the building. This sign should replace existing lettering or signs attached to the building. Existing signs should be removed when the new signs are installed or at a reasonable length of time coinciding with normal maintenance cycles.

Building identification signs should be placed in a consistent manner near major entrances. As a general rule the signs should be placed at right angles to the direction of traffic. If pathways are involved, the signs should be 6 ft clear of the edge and at least 6 ft in front of shrubbery or other landscape elements where possible.

If site conditions do not allow a sign to be located perpendicular to the building, then the sign location may be adjusted to a 45° angle or parallel to traffic.

- Design intent drawing: page 98

- Specification: pages 125–127

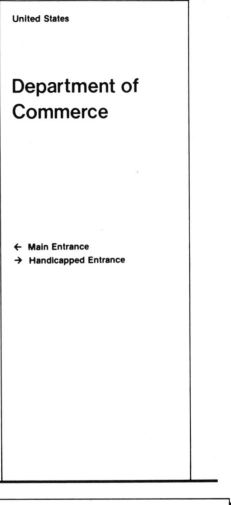

Facility Identification

PARKING LOT IDENTIFICATION

Location

The parking lot entrance should be identified with employee and/or visitor designation along with the facility name. Entrance and exits should be identified with appropriate information for the handicapped.

These signs should be located at least 6 ft before the specific lot entrance, placed perpendicular to traffic, and where possible, set back from the edge of the pavement a minimum of 6 ft.

- Design intent drawing: page 99

- Specification: pages 125–126

SITE DIRECTION/INFORMATION PROHIBITORY

Location

Directional signs for motorists should be located between 100 and 200 ft back from the intersection. Assuming the messages are large enough, this will provide the motorist with the opportunity to see the sign, read it, and make a driving decision (e.g., to change lanes or make any turn). These signs should be displayed at right angles to the direction of the traffic they are intended to serve and should be located 6 ft from the curb face. This may, in some instances, place the sign inside the municipal right-of-way, which will require that permission be obtained from local authorities to place it there.

Directional signs for pedestrians should be placed in parking lots, in plazas, and where highly traveled walkways intersect. The signs should be placed perpendicular to the flow of pedestrian traffic.

If signs on posts are accessible by pedestrians, a minimum of 7 ft from finished grade to bottom of sign panel is required; otherwise, 5 ft of grade clearance may be maintained. Wall-mounted signs should maintain a 5-ft distance from the bottom of the sign panel to the finished grade.

- Design intent drawing: pages 100–101

- Specification: pages 125–127

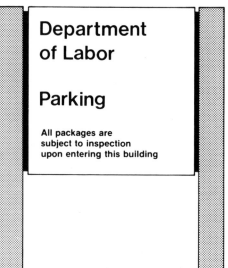

**(Left and below)
Parking lot identification**

United States

Department of Commerce Employee Parking

Department of Labor

Parking

All packages are subject to inspection upon entering this building

**Site direction/
information/
prohibitory** ▶

NOTICE:
All trucks sound
horn and wait for
signal to enter.

No trucks allowed
from 7:30 A.M. to
9:30 A.M.

↑
GSA Self Service
Store
Customer Entrance

→
Deliveries Only

Employee
Parking
Only

STOP

15
mph

Cafeteria
Service Drive

Permit Parking

Do not block driveway.
Unauthorized vehicles
will be towed away at
owners expense.

PARKING LOT DIRECTION/ INFORMATION

Location

Single-level parking lot signs should be located either on vertical wall surfaces or, if on posts, out of the path of vehicular circulation and perpendicular to traffic flow. If signs on posts are accessible to pedestrians, a minimum of 7 ft from the finished grade to the bottom of the sign panel is required; otherwise, 5 ft may be maintained. Wall-mounted signs should maintain a 5-ft distance from bottom of sign panel to finished grade.

Multilevel parking lot signs should be located at key decision points throughout the parking circulation path. A clearance from the finished grade to bottom of the sign panel should be maintained at a height equal to the established minimum clearance. *Signs should always be positioned perpendicular to traffic flow.*

Parking identification signs for the handicapped should be located in each parking space for the handicapped. If wall-mounted, the signs should be centered in the parking space width, a minimum of 5 ft 6 in from the finished grade to the bottom of the sign panel. If the sign is to be ceiling-hung, a minimum clearance of 7 ft from the finished grade to bottom of the sign is required.

- Design intent drawing: page 102
- Specification: pages 127–128

FACILITY DIRECTORIES

Location

Wall-mounted directories should be located in the facility's main entrance lobby or lobbies. Directories should be clearly visible to visitors as they enter the facility.

The exact location and size should be determined according to independent facility requirements. The height of the directory should be approximately 5 ft from the finished floor to the horizontal center line of the directory when possible.

Freestanding directories should be located in the main entrance lobby or lobbies. Their exact location will vary according to architectural layout. They should, however, be clearly visible to visitor traffic without obstructing circulation.

Use of freestanding signs (of any classification or type) should not be considered where they will cause a potential hazard to traffic.

- Design intent drawing: pages 104–105
- Specification: page 129

← First Level Parking	Exit First St. →
← Exit Second St.	

← First Level Parking Entrance

Parking for Wheelchair Handicapped Only

Parking lot direction and information

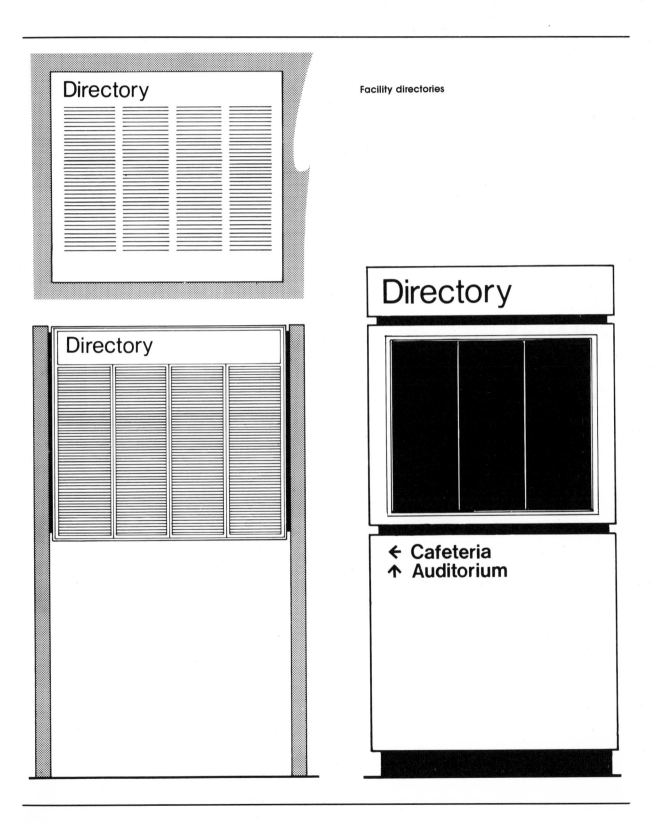

Facility directories

NOTICES/INFORMATION/REGULATIONS

Location

For the most part, these signs should be mounted
on a vertical surface. Care should be taken to
ensure a height sufficient to allow an unobstructed
view of the sign (average eye level is
approximately 5 ft to 5 ft 4 in from a finished floor).
The exact location should be determined on site
by the designer. The most important requirement
for location is to present the necessary information
at the point where the viewer is first exposed to it.

- Design intent drawing: pages 106–107

- Specification: page 130

In case of fire use exit stairs. Do not use Elevator.

Official notices regulations

ORIENTATION/FACILITY MAPS

Location

Interior facility maps should be located in close
proximity to, or as part of, the directory in the
main lobby. If maps are used on individual floors,
the maps should be located close to, or as part
of, floor directories.

It is important to position and orient floor-plan art
so that it accurately portrays the actual floor plan
as well as the viewer's location on the floor.

A "You Are Here" type of device may be used
on the map to identify the viewer's position on the
floor and in the building.

- Design intent drawing: page 103

- Specification: page 129

Orientation facility map ▶

Building Map

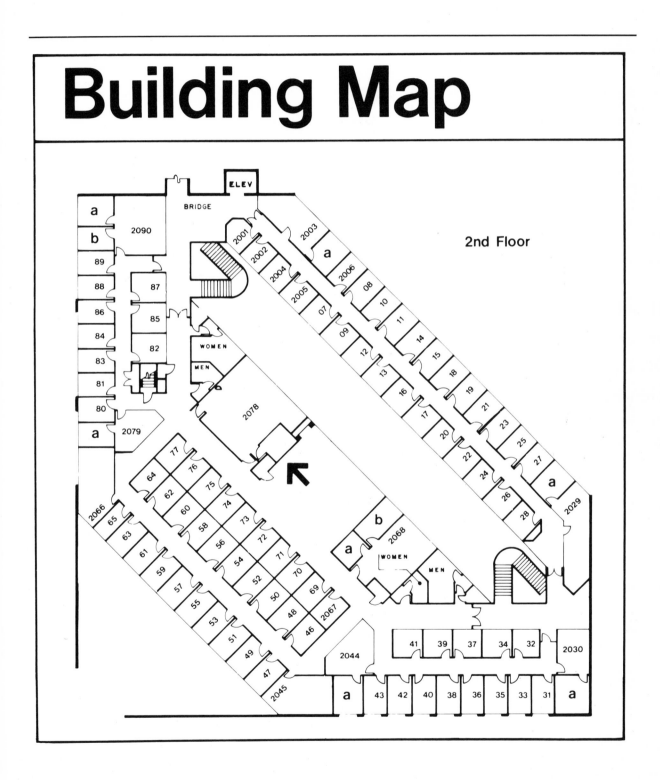

2nd Floor

NOTICES/INFORMATION/REGULATIONS

Location

Notice/information/regulations signs should be located at key points along the route of the visitor where specific instruction or information is required to assist the visitor. There is no set guide for locating this type of sign. Determination of sign location must be made during the facility walk-through either on site or on plan drawings.

Where appropriate, these signs should be positioned at the height of 5 ft 6 in from the finished floor to the top of the sign panel. There will be circumstances which dictate a higher or lower position. The decision should be made by the designer.

- Design intent drawing: pages 106–107

- Specification: page 130

REST ROOMS

Location

Rest room signs should be located on the rest room door, centered at a height of 5 ft 6 in from the finished floor to the top of the sign panel. Except for height, local conditions may dictate exception to location of the sign.

- Design intent drawing: page 108

- Specification: page 130

Absolutely no admittance. Cafeteria employees only.

Notices/information/regulations

Women

Rest rooms

Men

WARNING/PROHIBITORY

Location

These signs should be located at key points along the route of the visitor where specific warning or prohibitory information is required to control visitor activity.

There is no set guide for locating this type of sign. Determination must be made during facility walk-through either on site or on plan drawings.

Where appropriate, these signs should be positioned at a height of 5 ft 6 in from the finished floor to the top of the sign panel. There will be circumstances which dictate a higher or lower position. This decision should be made by the designer.

- Design intent drawings: page 109

- Specification: page 130

Warning/prohibitory

FACILITY SELF-PROTECTION PLAN

Location

These signs should be located in major public corridors and appropriately placed near elevators and/or stairways in sufficient quantities for maximum traffic exposure. The facility's management should determine exact location and quantities. The height of the signs from the finished floor to the bottom of the panel should be 4 ft.

- Design intent drawing: page 110

- Specification: page 129

Facility self-protection plan

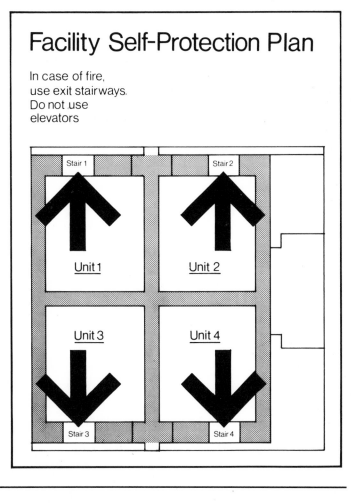

INTERIOR DIRECTIONAL

Location

Interior directional signs should be positioned 5 ft 6 in from the finished floor to the top of the sign panel. The distance in from the wall corners should be a minimum of 6 in.

- Design intent drawings: pages 111–112

- Specification: page 130

FLOOR AND STAIR IDENTIFICATION

Location

Floor identification signs should, where possible, be located in the elevator lobby of each floor where view is possible from the elevator cab with the door open. Floor identification may be made an integral part of floor directories.

These signs should be positioned 5 ft 6 in from the finished floor to the top of the sign panel.

To assist in emergency evacuation and floor circulation, it is recommended that inside of stairwells have floor number identification displayed at each level landing, 5 ft 6 in from the finished floor to the top of the sign. Height may vary according to different stairwell configurations.

It is also recommended that all stairs, in addition to existing illuminated exit signs, be identified with a stair number. This identification should be located on the corridor side of the door into the stairwell, centered at a height of 5 ft 6 in from the finished floor to the top of the sign.

- Design intent drawing: page 113

- Specification: page 130

←	
Administration and Records Division	3101
Assistant General Counsel	
Administration and Records Division	3103
Civil Rights	
Administration and Records Division	3104
	→
Assistant General Counsel	
Automated Data	
and Telecommunications Div.	3201
Equal Employment Opportunity Coordinator	
Management Planning Branch Chief	
Automated Data	
and Telecommunications Div.	3221

Interior directional

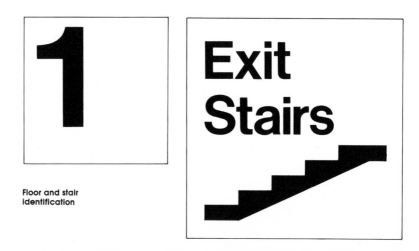

Floor and stair identification

FLOOR DIRECTORIES

Location

Floor directories should be located in the elevator lobbies of each respective floor, clearly visible to traffic entering the lobby area from elevators or corridors. A directory should be positioned a minimum of 4 ft from the finished floor to the bottom of the directory.

- Design intent drawing: pages 114–115

- Specification: pages 130–131

ROOM NUMBER

Room number signs are considered part of a facility's identification with or without the facility's function. Consideration must be given to possible future need for function to be added to a sign which initially needs only a number. Refer to office identification sign type in the catalog for room number.

Location

The room number sign shall be located on the wall at the closure (latch) side of the door when possible, 6 in from the outer edge of the door frame and 5 ft 6 in from the finished floor to the top of the sign panel.

Floor directories

3

Administration and Records Division	3101
Assistant General Counsel	
Administration and Records Division	3103
Civil Rights	
Administration and Records Division	3104
Assistant General Counsel	
Automated Data	
and Telecommunications Div.	3201
Equal Employment Opportunity Coordinator	
Management Planning Branch Chief	
Automated Data	
and Telecommunications Div.	3221

RMS 3101-3144   **RMS 3201-3241**

←   →

4th Floor

Division of Archives History & Record Mgt. Director	405
Documents	404

INVENTORY ROOM NUMBERING

Location

Nonpublic doors such as custodians' closets, electrical and mechanical rooms, telephone equipment rooms, etc., should not be identified with a standard room number sign plaque. They must, however, be assigned a room number within the room-numbering sequence for each floor of the facility. These numbers will correspond to the inventory system of all rooms.

These numbers are to be located in the upper right-hand corner of the door frame.

- Design intent drawing: page 116

- Specification: page 131

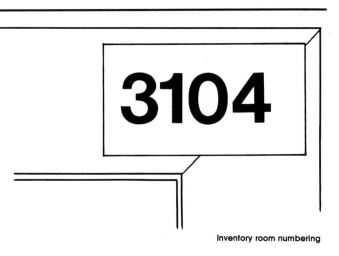

Inventory room numbering

OFFICE IDENTIFICATION

Location

Office identification signs should be located on the wall at the closure (latch) side of the door when possible, 6 in from the outer edge of the door frame and 5 ft 6 in from the finished floor to the top of the sign.

To accommodate the visually handicapped, numerals forming the room number should be raised ($1/32$ to $3/64$ in), or, if preferred, a separate clear or wall-color-matching raised room number, between $1/2$ and $3/4$ in high, may be located directly beneath and flush with the left edge of the sign plaque.

- Design intent drawing: pages 117–119

- Specification: pages 131–132

3103

Assistant General Counsel
Administration and Records Division

Office identification

PERSONNEL IDENTIFICATION

Location

These items should be located at the front of the desk, positioned at the left or right corner when possible.

In open planned areas, partition-mounted units should be located toward the outer corner of the partition closest to traffic circulation.

- Design intent drawing: page 121

- Specification: pages 131–132

John D. Smith
Assistant Director

Personnel Identification

BULLETIN BOARD

Location

Bulletin-board units should be located adjacent to major traffic accesses to floors, such as near elevator lobbies or stairs. The units should be positioned at a height of approximately 5 ft from the finished floor to the horizontal center line of the bulletin board.

- Design intent drawing: page 122

- Specification: page 133

Bulletin board

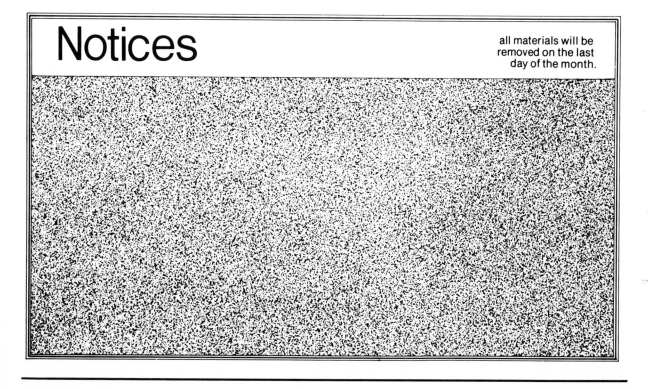

CHANGEABLE LETTER-BOARD/ IDENTIFICATION

Location

The changeable letter-board/identification sign may be desirable for situations requiring special programming of activities on a frequently changing basis. This sign basically functions as a room identification sign and should be located on the wall at the closure (latch) side of the door when possible, 6 in from the outer edge of the door frame and 5 ft 6 in from the finished floor to the top of the sign panel.

This type of unit may also be freestanding using a standard double T-base.

- Design intent drawing: page 123

- Specification: page 133

DISPLAY CASE

Location

Display cases may be required for historical documents such as the Constitution, Bill of Rights, and Declaration of Independence. These units may be freestanding or wall-mounted, exterior or interior, vertical or horizontal.

In new facilities, provision should be made for recessing a display case in a wall, located in the main lobby. If a freestanding unit is used, it must not interfere with or create a hazard to traffic flow.

In each situation, be it in a new or existing facility, the final location should be determined by the architect or designer.

- Design intent drawing: page 124

- Specification: pages 133–134

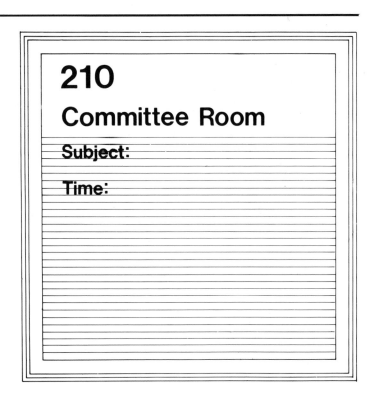

210
Committee Room

Subject:

Time:

Changeable letter board

Display case ▶

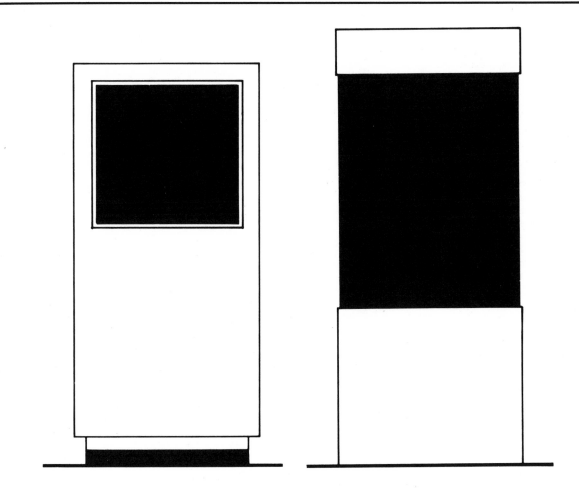

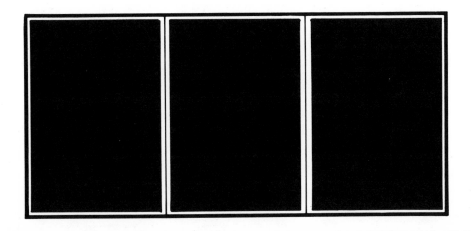

TEMPORARY SIGNS

Temporary signs should be used only when absolutely essential, because of such situations as temporary budget constraints, unavoidable schedule delays, or unexpected notice for an immediate need.

These signs should be removed when their function has been fulfilled or when a permanent sign has been put in place.

Temporary signs should be constructed in a manner, and within a budget, that takes account of the fact that they are not intended to remain up for more than 6 to 10 months. If it is intended that the sign will remain up for more than a year it should be installed as a permanent sign.

Graphics in a temporary sign should resemble those of the permanent signs. Hand lettering is to be avoided; if a silk-screen capability exists and it is the most practical method available, silk screening may be used. Usually the most practical method, however, is the use of die-cut vinyl graphics on painted panels or rub-on dry-transfer type.

Except where local conditions prevent it, the assumption is made that the facility's own staff should be capable of constructing and erecting/mounting all temporary signs.

Specific design and specifications for temporary signs are not included here. However, within budgetary constraints, every effort should be made to incorporate the functional design features of the permanent signage system.

ELEVATORS

Each elevator cab should have a "No Smoking" symbol located on the back wall of the cab, 6 ft. from the finished floor to the bottom of the sign panel.

In addition to the "No Smoking" symbol inside the elevator cab, it is recommended that a "No Smoking" sign also be located in each elevator lobby.

It is the responsibility of the elevator manufacturer to provide information on elevator passenger capacity, accommodations for the handicapped in the floor selector panel, and raised floor identification located on the right elevator doorjamb of each floor.

TRAFFIC CONTROL SIGNS

The design and use of all traffic control devices is governed by the Department of Transportation (DOT) *Manual of Uniform Traffic Control Devices*. The aim of achieving standardization in the area of regulatory warning and guide signs is beyond dispute, and the provisions of the manual must be followed closely. DOT is very specific on all matters relating to the dimensions and content of signs, their color, reflectorization, and the shape and sizes of letters.

While the manual is specific on the subject of placement, it does not prescribe any particular design for the support. Thus, in the interest of making all the supports in the system consistent in design, it is recommended that a design improved beyond the standard galvanized channel be used.

FABRICATION MATERIALS (SUPPLEMENTAL INFORMATION)

Adhesive Films

Adhesive films are thin sheets of vinyl or plastic with normally pressure-sensitive adhesive backings. Adhesive films are available in a wide variety of colors and finishes. Individual letters, messages, and symbols up to 12 in high are generally die-cut by either "steel rule" or thermal dies. Items larger than 12 in usually are hand-cut. This group also includes dry-transfer letters and decals (short for decalcomanias), which identifies a process of transferring preprinted images onto smooth, clean surfaces by either a pressure-sensitive or a water-activated adhesive.

Photographic Film and Paper

Photographic film and paper have only recently been applied to signage requirements and involve the use of specially designed cameras and processing equipment to produce the desired end product, whether it be *negative* (clear image on opaque background) or *positive* (opaque image on clear background) film, or *positive* (black image on white background) or *reverse* (white image on black background) paper prints.

Plastics

Plastics identifies the group of materials that is most frequently employed in sign production. Although there are many more, only nine plastic types are presently suitable to the broad range of signage applications. The generic name of these are (1) acrylics, (2) acrylic polyvinyl chlorides, (3) polyvinyl chlorides (PVC), (4) polycarbonates, (5) butyrates, (6) styrenes, (7) polypropylenes, (8) fiber-reinforced polyester (FRP), and (9) FRP-nylon.

The techniques that have been developed to best utilize these materials are known in the industry as vacuum-forming, molding, die-cutting, engraving, sandblasting, casting, and imbedding.

Wood

Wood is a natural product that because of the characteristics of its many species serves a broad range of signage applications. The great variety of grain patterns, coloration, and hardness available, plus its relatively easy workability, has made it one of the oldest and most widely used of all sign materials.

The selection of specific woods for both exterior and interior sign fabrication should be made from those generally used in architectural construction. To preserve the attributes for which any wood may be selected, it must be specially treated or coated according to its individual susceptibility to deterioration. This consideration may well bring the end-item cost of wood signs up to or even above some fabricated in other materials. The decision then becomes one of aesthetics versus economics, i.e., true cost-effectiveness.

Metals

Steel, aluminum, and bronze/brass are used in a variety of sign requirements. Galvanized (zinc-coated) steel is relatively inexpensive and is readily fabricated and easily welded.

Aluminum (by volume) is one-third the weight of steel and is nonrusting. It is available in a wide variety of extruded shapes and color finishes which meet many of the diverse requirements of sign fabrication.

Bronze and brass are bright alloys of copper, zinc, and small percentages of such metals as lead and nickel. They are most often cast, saw-cut, or extruded into sign plaques or sign components. These may be treated (coated) to inhibit surface oxidation but most often are not because this oxidation, whether chemically induced or natural, produces an aesthetically desirable patina.

Neon

Neon is the term generally used to describe several inert gases which when contained in a glass vacuum tube and subjected to an electrical current produce a specific color glow. Colors in addition to those characteristic of these gases are achieved by coating the inside of the glass tubes with a fluorescent powder or by using colored glass tubing.

Note: Since the use of "neon" is somewhat restricted to elaborate outdoor applications in highly specialized markets, and is generally considered to constitute a unique and independent "system," it is not detailed in this book.

Paper and Paperboard Products

Paper and paperboard products are generally confined to short-term or temporary sign uses. Specially formulated or treated papers serve as essential elements and/or "steps" in the production of permanent signage.

Stone and Masonry

Use of stone and masonry as sign materials is extremely limited and is generally confined to architectural or burial-ground applications.

TECHNIQUES (SUPPLEMENTAL INFORMATION)

Hot Stamping

Hot stamping employs metal type in conjunction with sheets of film or foil. The type is electrically heated and, under controlled pressure, transfers the message onto the receiving surface, literally fusing or "branding" the selected characters into it. Hot stamping is applicable to requirements for small type sizes, such as personnel name plaques and changeable message strips.

Silk Screening

Silk screening is a method that employs a stencil, either hand-cut or photo-processed, that is transferred into a framed panel of tautly stretched, fine-mesh silk. When the positive image is dissolved out and the clogged background area of the screen has dried, specially prepared ink paste is applied through the open areas of the screen onto the receiving surface. A different, precisely registered screen is required for each color used. Silk screening is most effective for requirements where large areas and/or two or more colors are used, such as symbol/signs, pictographs, orientation maps, etc., and especially when subsurface or imbedded graphics are indiciated.

Coatings

Coatings perform specific functions and are applied to nearly all sign materials. Acrylics, alkyds, asphalts, epoxys, esters, latexes, oils, oleoresins, phenolics, silicons, urethanes, varnishes, and vinyls are some of those most frequently used. These substances preserve, seal, inhibit fading, control reflectance, and provide surface textures. Because of their close working relationships with the manufacturers of bulk materials, sign fabricators are best qualified to make recommendations regarding specific coating applications. It should be noted here that

an increasing number of these established fabricators offer a range of signs in several configurations, materials, and color combinations that they identify as sign systems. Although the workmanship and concepts embodied in these are generally quite excellent, they are not sign systems in the context of this book, which signals a far broader requirement than can be met totally by such off-the-shell items alone. However, consideration of these available systems for their demonstrated styles, materials, and fabrication techniques, upon which a discrete signage system may be cost-effectively developed, is strongly recommended.

PART THREE

Procurement:
The Last Step

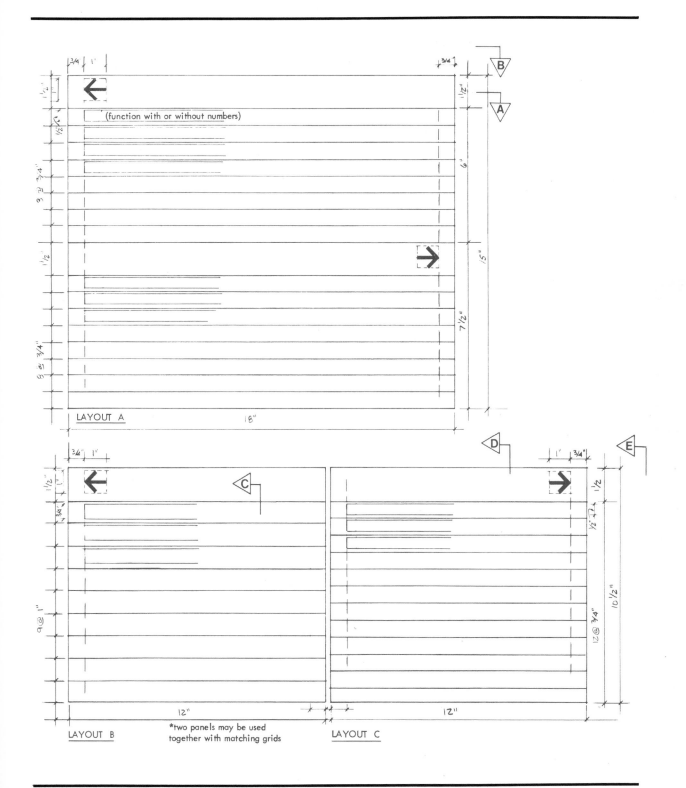

(function with or without numbers)

LAYOUT A

LAYOUT B

*two panels may be used
together with matching grids

LAYOUT C

CHAPTER EIGHT

Elements of a Contract Package

We often think that when we have completed our study of ONE we know about TWO, because "two" is "one and one." We forget that we still have to make a study of "and."

—A. Eddington,
The Nature of Physics

The U.S. General Services Administration (GSA) is the landlord, housekeeper, and supply and maintenance manager for nearly 10,000 buildings utilized by the federal government's civilian agencies. Supplying the signage for those facilities has become still another item added to the already long list of services the GSA must provide for itself and its "tenants."

There are several volumes of procurement regulations (PRs) that spell our responsibilities and procedures covering every facet and contingency of doing business by, for, and with the federal government. Professional contract administrators, legal specialists, and specification writers have developed appropriate standard forms (SF's) which translate the applicable PR's into contract general conditions (boiler plate), which are assembled into and become an integral part of each request for proposal (RFP), each invitation for bid (IFB), and contracts that the GSA issues.

This process, known as "solicitation, offer, and award," is illustrated here in outline form. It is important to note that equivalent commercial procedures are generally far less complicated and time-consuming. Nevertheless, the federal government's contracting instruments represent a totality from which simplified, effective commercial contract models can be fashioned.

Assuming that a need for signage or a signage system has been identified, one of the following programs is initiated:

Note: Although this is the federal government's standard procedure for selecting an architect/ engineer (A/E), it appears to be equally applicable for selecting a graphic design consultant. Both are in professional disciplines of seemingly equal stature.

A/E Selection/Award Network

1. Develop request for A/E fee proposal.
2. Legal review contract.
3. Appoint A/E evaluation board.
4. Prepare A/E interview package.
5. Prepare announcement and letter for publication in the *Commerce Business Daily (CBD).*
6. Send announcement to CBD and publish.
7. Receive applications and SF 255's.
8. Prepare briefing.
9. Pull SF 254's from file.
10. Evaluate and recommend A/E's.
11. Set time, place, and date of interviews.
12. Prepare announcement of Public Advisory Panel (PAP) recommendation.
13. Provide evaluation team with interview package.
14. Brief evaluation team.
15. Advise A/E's and send interview package.
16. Publish PAP recommendation in *CBD.*
17. Distribute PAP recommendation in central office.
18. A/E's prepare presentations.
19. Interview and rank A/E's.
20. Prepare memo recommending selection.
21. Forward recommendation to regional administrator.
22. Schedule preaward audit.
23. Select A/E.
24. Advise region of selection.
25. Advise selected A/E.
26. Notify nonselected A/E's.
27. Request A/E fee proposal.
28. Prepare government fee estimate.
29. Appoint negotiation committee.
30. A/E prepares proposal.
31. Develop negotiation position and plan.
32. Start preaward audit.
33. Make technical evaluation of proposal.
34. Complete preaward audit.
35. Review all documents and adjust estimate.
36. Establish negotiation date and advise A/E.
37. Conduct negotiations.
38. Award contract.

Note: Total estimated optimum duration of this procedure is 97 working days (135 calendar days).

THE PROCUREMENT CYCLE

Note: The procedure is separated into three phases: presolicitation, solicitation/award, and postaward administration. They will be referred to simply as phase 1, phase 2, and phase 3 in the following outline of actions and events that constitute the general procurement cycle.

Phase 1 (presolicitation)

1. Individual identifies a procurement need, thus establishing the requirement.

2. The procurement request is made up of:
   a. Schedule/statement of work
   b. Specifications
   c. Drawings
   d. Delivery dates
   e. Special conditions
   f. Any necessary approvals from higher authority
   g. Other (if required)
   h. Cost estimates (in-house)

3. The request then goes to:
   a. Approving authority

b. Requirements review

c. Specifications writer (usually technical)

The presolicitation work is completed when the person with need submits the package to the budget officer who certifies the availability of and commits the requested funds for the program/ project.

Phase 2 (solicitation/award)

Depending upon the nature of the projected procurement, the contracting officer (CO), together with initiating officer, legal (if required), and technical advisers to the CO, will prepare a solicitation document for either formal advertising, or invitation for bid (IFB), or negotiation, or request for proposal (RFP).

Inputs for IFB are:

1. Review PR, e.g.,
   a. Specifications are clear and not contradictory or restrictive.
   b. Delivery schedule is realistic.
   c. There is familiarization with technical details.

2. Determine that conditions for formal advertising are present.
   a. Define specifications.
   b. Ensure adequate number of suppliers.
   c. Ensure adequate time.

3. Prepare IFB, including:
   a. Control and administrative information.
   b. Specifications (or information on where to obtain).
   c. Any special bidding conditions, e.g., alternate bids, small business, price escalation, special qualifications.

4. Assemble solicitation list. Maximize full and free competition.

5. Synopsize as required.

6. Ensure that amendments and extra information are furnished to all invitees.

Inputs for RFP are:

1. Review PR (as in formal advertising).

2. Justify negotiation under 41 USC 252.

3. Obtain necessary approvals, including Findings and Determinations (F & D), if required.

4. Prepare source list and coordinate it with requiring personnel as necessary.

5. Determine pricing arrangement on a tentative basis: cost-reimbursement or fixed-price.

6. Determine patent, data, and copyright arrangements.

7. Determine what Government Furnished Property (GFP) is required and its availability.

8. Determine requirements for cost information from proposers.

9. Synopsize as required.

10. Obtain legal and technical approvals as required.

11. Distribute RFP.

12. Ensure that amendments and extra information are furnished to all invitees.

13. Schedule proposal meeting, if any.

The results of the solicitation are then evaluated.

In the case of *formal advertising* the inputs are:

1. Open and read bids at appointed time.

2. Prepare abstract.

3. Arrange for examination of bids and abstract, if requested.

4. Determine responsibility for lateness of any bids or modifications.

5. Note possible mistakes in bids and follow correct procedure.

6. Determine responsiveness of bids.

7. Determine low bid.

8. Determine low bidder's responsibility.

9. Receive and resolve any protests.

In the case of negotiation the inputs are:

1. Review offers to ensure that:
   a. All questions are answered.
   b. Price breakdowns are included as required.
   c. Arithmetic is correct.
   d. Award deadline is specified.
   e. All amendments are accepted.
   f. Offerer's exceptions are referred to appropriate official for decision.

2. Obtain technical evaluation of offers.

3. Obtain cost, price, and profit analysis as required.

4. Do business evaluation.

5. Select offerers to negotiate with.

6. Determine responsibility of offerers selected for negotiation.

The next step is negotiation. Here, the contracting officer and the negotiating team will perform the following prenegotiation actions:

1. Obtain information on offerer, particularly:
   a. Department and personnel who will perform the contract.
   b. Names of officers, representatives, and negotiators.
   c. Location where work will be performed.
   d. Availability of personnel who will perform the work.
   e. Need for any government financing.
   f. A review of offerer's make-or-buy program and purchasing and accounting systems.
   g. An evaluation of need for GFP.

In the negotiation appropriate techniques will be used to:

1. Evaluate offerer's position and estimates.

2. Set forth the government's position.

3. Explore alternatives in case of disagreement.

4. Make sure that all important issues are resolved and understood by both parties.

Next, the contracting officer, with the approval of the proper authorities and the budget office, will:

1. Obtain necessary clearances.

2. Execute the award/contract.

3. Notify unsuccessful bidders/offerers.

4. Publicize award in *CBD*, if required.

5. Obligate funds.

Phase 3 (postaward administration)

In the final phase the contracting officer and/or authorized representative will perform the following functions in administering the contract:

1. Obtain progress information as required:
   a. Schedule.
   b. Review monthly production progress reports.
   c. Review material inspection and receiving reports.
   d. Review progress reports.
   e. Review financial management report.
   f. Review cost incurred on contract report.
   g. Review program evaluation and reporting technique (PERT), if required
   h. Review labor-management information.

2. Avoid informal commitments to contractor.

3. Follow appropriate procedures for changes and contract modifications.

During this phase the contracting officer along with inspection/receiving, material, and the office of finance will monitor to completion, make formal acceptance and payment, or if circumstances dictate, the contracting officer, together with legal counsel and cost/price analysts, will request

a termination of the contract. If the termination is for convenience the following actions will be performed:

1. Obtain necessary approvals.

2. Assess effect on
   a. Budget and funds.
   b. Subsidiary and related requirements.
   c. Requirements of other activities.

3. Notify contractor, *avoiding advance leaks.*

4. Screen termination inventory.

5. Negotiate settlement.

6. Make equitable adjustment for contract, if any.

If the termination is made because of default, the following actions will be performed:

1. Determine if grounds exist for default.

2. Obtain necessary approvals.

3. Notify contractor.

4. Prepare for appeal under disputes clause.

For comparison with the government's approach, the commercial design process, extracted from the Michigan Council for the Arts' *Client Guide for Signage and Architectural Graphics,* is offered. It is exemplary of the process and can readily be modified to accommodate most individual project requirements.

Preplanning

1. Client defines the project scope, budget, and schedule and collaborates with the designer in determining their respective responsibilities.

2. Designer outlines the design objectives, and prepares a work schedule and a cost estimate of design services.

3. Designer submits fee estimates, time schedule, and contractual agreement to client for approval.

4. Client reviews and approves fee estimates, time schedule, and contractual agreement.

Programming

1. Client provides information about types of users, any projected changes and needed flexibility, maintenance procedures, and special requirements such as security.

2. Designer establishes the priorities of information (primary, secondary, directional, safety warning, miscellaneous) and determines sites or points at which users make directional decisions.

3. Designer establishes criteria for legibility, placement, wording, flexibility, purchasing, and maintenance. A written presentation of these program criteria is submitted to the client.

4. Client reviews and approves the program criteria.

Preliminary Design

1. Designer investigates letter styles, use of color, use of symbols, formats, hardware and mounting systems, lighting systems, finishes, fabrication techniques, and proposed placement of signs.

2. Designer presents the proposal options in sketch, diagram, and model form.

3. Client reviews and approves the preliminary design proposals, proposed wording, and sign placement.

Final Design

1. Client develops final copy with designer.

2. Designer selects letter styles, colors, formats, hardward and mounting systems, lighting arrangements, finishes, and fabrication techniques.

3. Designer obtains fabrication cost estimates, as required.

4. Designer presents the final proposals in finished form with drawings, models, and/or prototypes, materials, and color samples.

5. Client checks the final proposal against program criteria and approves.

Documentation

1. Designer provides the complete working drawings and specifications (manual) for all signing items, including colors, materials, formats, lighting finishes, and fabrication techniques.

2. Designer provides final placement plans and graphic schedule of all items.

3. Client approves working drawings and specifications.

4. Designer recommends competent bidders as necessary, issues bid documents, and reviews them with bidders. He or she then assists the client with bid negotiations.

Production

1. Client contacts suppliers, fabricators, and installers for contract bids. Client reviews and selects bidders according to needs and recommendations of the designer.

2. Designer checks shop drawings, inspects work in the fabricator's shop, and observes installation at the project site.

3. Designer revises the signage manual for maintenance of the system, if required.

Of further interest is a somewhat more detailed flowchart, which clearly establishes not only similarities in design-process thinking between members of the professional graphic design community, but also the advisability of their introduction to the signage program at the earliest practical point.

Planning

1. Define scope:
   a. Interior
   b. Exterior
   c. Interface
   d. Roadway

2. Define consultant's responsibilities:
   a. Input
   b. Coordination
   c. Design
   d. Documentation
   e. Management

3. Define owner's responsibilities:
   a. Input
   b. Budget
   c. Coordination
   d. Approvals

4. Define continuing signage management.

5. Define installation and maintenance procedures.
   From the foregoing, define parameters and secure approval.

Programming

1. Establish priorities of information:
   a. Primary
   b. Secondary
   c. Directional
   d. Identification
   e. Regulatory
   f. Informational
   g. Miscellaneous

2. Establish legibility criteria.

3. Establish placement criteria.

4. Establish typical wording parameters.

5. Establish flexibility criteria.

6. Establish leaseholders' criteria.

7. Establish in-house management.

8. Establish purchasing criteria.

9. Establish OSHA requirements.

10. Establish material availability.

11. Establish in-house fabrication capabilities.

12. Establish maintenance aspects criteria.

13. Establish technical committee requirements.
    Upon approval of this written program, *preliminary design* is developed through the following actions:
    1. Investigate letter styles.

    2. Investigate terminology.

    3. Investigate symbology.

    4. Investigate use of color.

5. Investigate legend/ground possibilities.

6. Investigate legibility factors.

7. Investigate modular system.

8. Investigate grid system.

9. Investigate materials and processes (prototype).

10. Investigate possible in-house fabrication.

11. Investigate hardward and mounting possibilities.

12. Investigate price.
    From these make a presentation of sketch concepts for approval. When approval is received, proceed with design; e.g.:
    1. Select letter style.

    2. Determine terminology.

    3. Determine symbology.

    4. Determine use of color.

    5. Determine legend/ground relationships.

    6. Determine legibility standards.

    7. Determine modular system.

    8. Determine grid system.

    9. Select materials and fabrication processes (obtain models).

    10. Determine if in-house fabrication is recommended.

    11. Determine all hardware (mounting details).

    12. Determine price.
        Make presentation and secure approvals before proceeding with documentation of:
        1. Unit drawings

        2. Details

        3. Specifications

        4. Placement drawings

        5. Location/terminology matrix

After approval of the bid package is obtained, a contract can be awarded to the successful bidder (assuming no in-house fabrication).

Subsequent to award, contract administration will include but not be limited to the following:

1. Approval of shop drawings

2. Manufacture of final system

3. Delivery of finished materials and hardware

4. Installation of system

Operation will consist largely of continuing implementation.

With the exception of A/E's (to date), every U.S. government procurement, whether in the nature of a fixed-price bid or a negotiated contract that is estimated to exceed 5000 dollars, must, by law, be advertised in the *Commerce Business Daily,* which is issued five days a week and lists specific business proposals for products and services wanted or offered by the U.S. government.

There are 19 letter codes for services and 77 number codes for supplies and equipment. Graphic design consultants will find announcements of interest under code H, for expert and consulting services. Signage fabricators will find announcements of interest under code 99, for miscellaneous supplies and services.

Note: There is no commercial equivalent to the federal government's *CBD* notice of commercial signage requirements. They are either uncovered by enterprising salespersons, spread by word of mouth, or, as is most often the case, known via direct solicitation by the prospective user/client.

Whatever programming model is developed, it is entirely likely that the procurement of graphic design and fabrication/installation services will closely parallel the essential considerations of the U.S. government's procurement instruments.

Under the phrasing "solicitation, offer, and award," the first of these is the *request for proposal (RFP),* for design services.

In addition to identifying the subject and inviting the recipient's submission of an offer, the solicitation package will contain the following parts:

1. General provisions (standard forms containing all policies and regulations applicable to the intended procurement). *Note:* since changes, amendments, deletions, and additions are constantly being introduced to these general provisions, it is strongly recommended that they be read and understood before responding to any solicitation issued by a federal, state, or local governmental agency.

2. Solicitation instructions and conditions.

3. Supplemental provisions modifications.

4. Special provisions; detailed statements of:
   a. Work to be performed.
   b. Responsibilities and obligations.
   c. Content, organization, and form of proposal, i.e., technical and price.
   d. Time, place, and conditions of award.

5. Proposal evaluation criteria:
   a. Technical qualifications.
   b. Experience.
   c. Physical rescources.
   d. Sample evaluation form.

6. Solicitation, offer, and award (standard form to be executed and returned with proposal).

7. Identification tag (to be affixed to sealed offer).

The second procurement instrument is the *invitation for bid (IFB).* This is developed or finalized, under the contract, resulting from the RFP, by the graphic design consultant.

The invitation package will contain a notice to the bidder explaining representations and certifications, the composition of the documents, and the following components:

1. Special conditions, including detailed statements of:
   a. Work to be performed.
   b. Responsibilities and obligations.
   c. Time and place of prebid conference.
   d. Time, place, and conditions of award.

2. Specifications (every detail necessary to ensure fulfillment of design concept and intent within established schedules of time and funds).

3. Contract drawings (design drawings of all sign types included in the contract).

4. Message schedules (exact copy for each sign).

5. Unit price bid list (a listing of all signs by type, specification number, and quantity whereon the unit, total, and aggregate bid price is to be entered).

Any IFB for signage fabrication should include but not be limited to the following special conditions:

1. The fabricator shall base his or her proposal on the performance of all services, including all items of labor, materials, and equipment required for the complete fabrication and installation of the specified work.

2. The fabricator shall furnish anchor, fastenings, attachment metals, and other miscellaneous metal items imbedded in concrete or building-wall material as required so as not to delay job progress.

3. The fabricator shall carefully study the detailed drawings for the various signs and make specific recommendations and changes if those changes will improve the quality of any sign. Such recommendations and changes shall be approved in writing by the contracting officer, or his or her technical representative, prior to preparation of shop drawings or fabrication of any samples or signs.

4. The fabricator shall carefully study the drawings and be responsible for the correct direction of all arrows on all signs, and for requesting a change of spacing if a message is too long to fit on the intended sign panel.

5. The following 1-year *guarantee*, from the date of final acceptance of the complete installation, shall apply to the following sign system characteristics. There shall be:
   a. No delamination of any of the parts of the signs or of the lettering from the sign face.
   b. No cupping, warping, or dishing in excess of the requirements stipulated in the specifications.
   c. No bubbling, crazing, chalking, rusting, or other disintegration of the sign face or of the messages or of the edge finish of the panels.
   d. No corrosion developing beneath paint surfaces of the support systems—except as the result of obvious vandalism or other external damage to those paint surfaces.
   e. No corrosion of the fastenings.
   f. No movement of signs from their foundations. The signs must remain true and plumb on their foundations—except when the sign has sustained obvious postinstallation external damage.
   g. No fading of the colors when matched against a sample of the original color and material.

6. The fabricator shall be required to provide final art. All typesetting required shall be by the phototype process.

7. The fabricator shall provide identification of all materials used, by manufacturer's descriptive literature, control number, name, code number, batch, and formula when available.

8. The fabricator shall provide a written maintenance schedule for all items he or she furnishes to accomplish cleaning, replacement, and repairs for the client.

9. The fabricator shall ensure that the design of all support structures and structural connections required for the performance of the work meet the requirements of the contract.

10. All bonded or fabricated panels shall have faces of such flatness that when measured from corner to corner along the diagonal, the maximum deviation from the nominal plane of the surface shall not exceed $1/16$ in for measured distances up to 5 ft.

11. Fastenings:
    a. Fastenings on sign-face surface of sign panels shall not be exposed, except where noted.
    b. Sign-face surfaces shall not be penetrated during fabrication or installation of signs, except where noted.
    c. Sign-face surfaces shall not be deformed, distorted, or discolored by attachment of concealed fastenings.
    d. All fastenings shall be resistant to oxidation or other corrosive action because of their composition, completely through their cross sections.
    e. Work shall be secured with fastenings of the same color and finish as the components they secure, where they are exposed to view.
    f. Fabrication work with fastenings shall be utilized in strict accordance with their manufacturer's specifications, directions, and recommendations, and as indicated on design intent drawings.

12. All work required under this contract shall be performed by specialists. (See "Bidder Qualification Guidelines" in procurement process summary.)

HOW TO PREPARE

Message/Location Schedules

The figure opposite provides a complete listing of all messages and graphic elements which are to be applied to the various sign panels. All information that is in parentheses ( ) shall not be considered part of the message. Phrasing of messages (words per line) shall be indicated in the message schedules. The use of (a) and (b) within the message panel will indicate the use of more than one weight of type style.

- The "Sign No." is determined from the location plans, starting with No. 1 for the first sign required and continuing the sequence through the total number of signs. All identical signs should be given the same number. Example: All "Men" signs might be No. 18.

- "Quantity" is the number of signs of a specific sign number.

- "Specification No." refers to the particular specification number for a sign as described in Chapter 10, "Technical Specifications."

- "Design Intent Drawing No." refers to the number shown at the bottom of the design intent drawings or the drawing number assigned by the user in the lower-right-hand box of the title block.

- "Location Plan No." refers to the specific architectural drawing plan on which a sign location has been indicated.

- "Grid No." refers to the design intent drawing containing a specific layout grid for a particular sign.

- "Color" refers to background color (B), message color (M).

- "Punch List Date" provides a means to inventory signs completed during installation inspection.

- "S/F" and "D/F" refer to single- or double-faced signs.

- Sign location drawings are provided as a guide to the fabricator. The sign locations shown approximate positions for individual items. The design intent drawings indicate exact location of certain signs. All others should be located on site by the designer with the fabricator/installer. Any discrepancies or deviations from the drawing locations due to different site conditions should be brought to the attention of the designer for solution.

- Sign location plans should be prepared in final form similar to the method described in the material on facility walk-through in Chapter 4.

Cost Estimates

The first step in preparing a cost estimate is to determine the quantities of the various sign types needed, the type size, copy, quantity, sign size, basic material/graphic application, and mounting. Such factors as internal illumination and single- or double-faced signs are also important.

The next step is to compile a catalog of sign costs for sign types which closely fit the profile of the signs required. Multiplying the sign unit cost by the quantity will provide a reasonable estimate. In addition, such factors as time required, state sales tax, installation, and freight costs have to be considered. Sign fabricators will be the most reliable sources for this information.

For a quick, rule-of-thumb estimate, approximately 20 cents per square foot of building area to be signed can be used for a preliminary estimate of the overall budget. It must be realized, however, that this is only a rough-estimate guide. A smaller building may require considerably more signs than a larger building, depending on the internal configuration and functional utilization.

Catalog of Costs

The catalog of costs will relate directly to the sign items listed in Chapter 7, "Catalog of Signs." The costs are based on a reasonable average price determined from quoted prices from various sign fabricators. These costs do not reflect shipping, installation, or sales taxes. Shipping and installation costs will depend on the fabricator's location relationship to the job site or sites.

The costs to be entered here will reflect unit costs based on a quantity of 1. Where multiples of the same sign are required, the unit cost may be reduced.

These costs will need to be revised on an annual basis, at minimum. Material and labor costs are ever-changing, which will render prices over a year old unreliable.

Message schedule ▶

Message Schedule

G.7

Sign No.

| Quantity: 1 | Punch List Date: 10-18-78 |
| Specification No. 2.12 | Grid Drawing No. 14-B |

Design Intent Drawing No. 11

Location Plan No. 3

| Color | B Ivory | M Black |

Message:

⟵ G 4 - G 50
⟵ G 200 - G 250
⟵ G 300 - G 355

| S/F | X | D/F | | Illuminated | | Non-Illuminated | X |

G.8

Sign No.

| Quantity: 7 | Punch List Date: 10-18-78 |
| Specification No. 2.11 | Grid Drawing No. 12-A |

Design Intent Drawing No. 13

Location Plan No. 3

| Color | B Ivory | M Black |

Message:

(Restroom symbol)
Women

| S/F | X | D/F | | Illuminated | | Non-Illuminated | X |

Sign type	Unit cost*	"Blank cost"
Building identification	$ _____	$ _____
Parking lot identification	_____	_____
Site direction/information/ prohibitory	_____	_____
Parking lot direction/ information	_____	_____
Official notices/ regulations	_____	_____
Building directories	_____	_____
Orientation/building maps	_____	_____
Notices/information/ regulations	_____	_____
Restrooms/symbols	_____	_____
Warning/prohibitory	_____	_____
Facility self-protection plan	_____	_____
Interior directional	_____	_____
Floor/stair identification	_____	_____
Floor directories	_____	_____
Room number	_____	_____
Inventory room numbering	_____	_____
Office identification	_____	_____
Personnel identification	_____	_____
Bulletin boards	_____	_____
Changeable letter-board identification	_____	_____
Display case	_____	_____

*To be determined prior to final contract documentation.

Order of Funding Priorities

Unfortunately, all too often signage budgets for buildings either are overlooked initially or are the first items to be reduced or eliminated when the building construction budget faces significant overrun. This situation presents management with the problem of reducing sign requirements. Without a defined set of guidelines for priorities of signs, any effort to implement use of some signs may be futile if what is installed is not complete enough to function alone.

Where to break up the overall system due to shortages of funds? First, the building's essential functional requirements for safety and traffic control must be provided, i.e., signs for building identification, no smoking, exit, handicapped accessibility, major directional devices, regulations and warning devices, building directory, and room numbers.

The second level of priorities deals with directional devices for pedestrian and vehicular traffic and the building occupant functions, i.e., room identification, area identification, personnel identification, and floor directories.

A further breakdown could be by floors according to established priorities of importance of functions on each floor.

Final Artwork and Typesetting

Final artwork for various sign items should be available from either of two sources. For federal facilities, GSA regional offices should provide available art for government seals and federally approved symbols. In both the federal and private sectors the designer, whether an in-house or professional consultant, is responsible for guidelines and/or artwork for special items within the system to be used.

The sign fabricator can be required to provide art for typefaces, spacing, color, and final delineation of the designer's specific artwork.

When colors are submitted for approval, it is important to require the manufacturer's identification of the color for future color matching.

Phototypesetting for all sign-message art is required. In contrast to cast metal type, which is locked into a fixed letter spacing format, phototypesetting offers greater control of proportional letter spacing as letter sizes are increased or decreased.

Contract Package Evaluation

This is the last critical point where the services of a professional graphics designer are required (contingent, of course, upon a local decision as to the facility's size/qualification).

The completed contract package should be thoroughly examined and adjusted as necessary to ensure clarity and completeness prior to issuance.

From this point, the following tasks remain to be performed: The procurement process:

- Solicitation for bids or negotiation
- Contract award
- Fabrication inspection
- Installation inspection
- Postinstallation evaluation

THE PROCUREMENT PROCESS SUMMARY

Procurement Time Scheulde

Establishing a standard time schedule for the procurement of signs is most difficult. There are often too many variables, such as the quantities of signs required and the diverse conditions that exist among the many qualified fabricators. In addition, individual client time requirements for solicitation and award of contracts vary significantly.

The following time schedule estimates should provide a reasonable rule of thumb for determining the approximate time required for bidding, fabrication, and installation of various-size projects. It is assumed that contract documents are complete and ready for issuance.

Function	Min. time, weeks	Max. time, weeks
1. Advertise for bids	2	4
2. Bid period	4	6
3. Contract award	2	4
4. Shop drawing/sample submittals from notice to proceed	3	4
5. Fabrication	4	12–16
6. Installation (both fabrication and installation time will vary according to project size, distance from fabricator to job site, and degree of staggered installation, if required)	1	4

Bidder Qualification Guidelines

The bidder, or the subcontractor that the bidder will use for performance of the work, should have had at least 3 years' successful experience in producing and installing signs.

In addition, the bidder or subcontractor shall have installed, on at least two prior projects, signs which are comparable to those required for the specific project required and which have been in use for a period of not less than 1 year.

A list of the prior comparable installations by the bidder or the subcontractor, together with the names and addresses of the buildings, the names of the owners or managers thereof, and any other pertinent information required shall be submitted promptly upon request of the client.

The names, addresses, experience, and a statement of the work performed by each subcontractor or second-tier subcontractor whom the bidder or the principal subcontractor wishes to use for performance of minor portions of the work, shall also be submitted promptly upon request of the client.

Bids may be rejected if the bidder has established on former jobs, either government, municipal, or commercial, a record of unsatisfactory work and installations; has repeatedly failed to complete contracts awarded within the contract time; or otherwise fails to meet the experience requirements of this clause.

The term *specialist* as used in the specification shall mean an individual or firm of established reputation (or if newly organized, whose personnel have previously established a reputation in the same field) which is regularly engaged in and maintains a regular force of workers skilled in either

manufacturing or fabrication (as applicable) of items required by the contract, or otherwise performing work required by the contract. Where the contract specification requires installation by a specialist, that term shall also be deemed to mean either the manufacturer of the item, or an individual or firm who will perform the work under the manufacturer's direct supervision.

Solicitation for Bids

Follow the current standard format for bid solicitation.

Contract Awards

Follow the current contract award procedure.

Shop Drawing/Sample Submissions

This task should be administered by the specific project coordinator or architect if one is involved. Standard procedures for review and approval should be followed.

Fabrication/Installation

Periodic policing of fabrication and installation should be conducted by the client's staff to ensure adherence to the intended design and quality control.

Postinstallation evaluation

This exercise is very important to the client's staff whose responsibility it is to deal with future sign projects. Thorough evaluation of the installed system of signs should be made with emphasis on the following:

- Performance of fabricator

- Performance of client's staff

- Cooperation of facility's tenants

- Success or failure of project schedule

- Trouble spots of fabrication/installation

- Effectiveness of cost estimating

- Acceptance and reaction to sign system in terms of functions and aesthetic compatibility.

Replacement/Maintenance

Each buyer of signs, whether small or large, should require the selected fabricator to provide a complete repair, replacement, and maintenance schedule, in writing, to the building manager or the contracting officer. Included in this schedule should be unit pricing of components, delivery time, repairability factors for those signs which it is determined feasible to repair, and general instructions for cleaning and servicing signs.

CHAPTER NINE

Design Intent Drawings

Design intent drawings show design intended for each sign type. The details reflect the minimum acceptable level of sign quality and performance. Optional details are shown where available. These options are not to be considered as an upgrade or downgrade of quality, but rather another way of fabrication which may be more appropriate in certain cases.

These drawings may be used as they are to indicate final detailing of materials, fasteners, and graphic application processes, or they may be used as a drawing content guide for the designer. Under no circumstances should they be used for fabrication of signs.

Note: The molded fiber glass monolithic facility identification sign shown on page 98 was developed by the author (C. H. B. McLendon) with Peter Masters from an original design by David Pesanelli of David Pesanelli Associates. Although many of the signage designs in these pages were created for federal facility application, several were taken from already existing standards developed by established sign fabrication firms.

Dimensions are shown in inches and should be converted to centimeters wherever the metric system is standard.

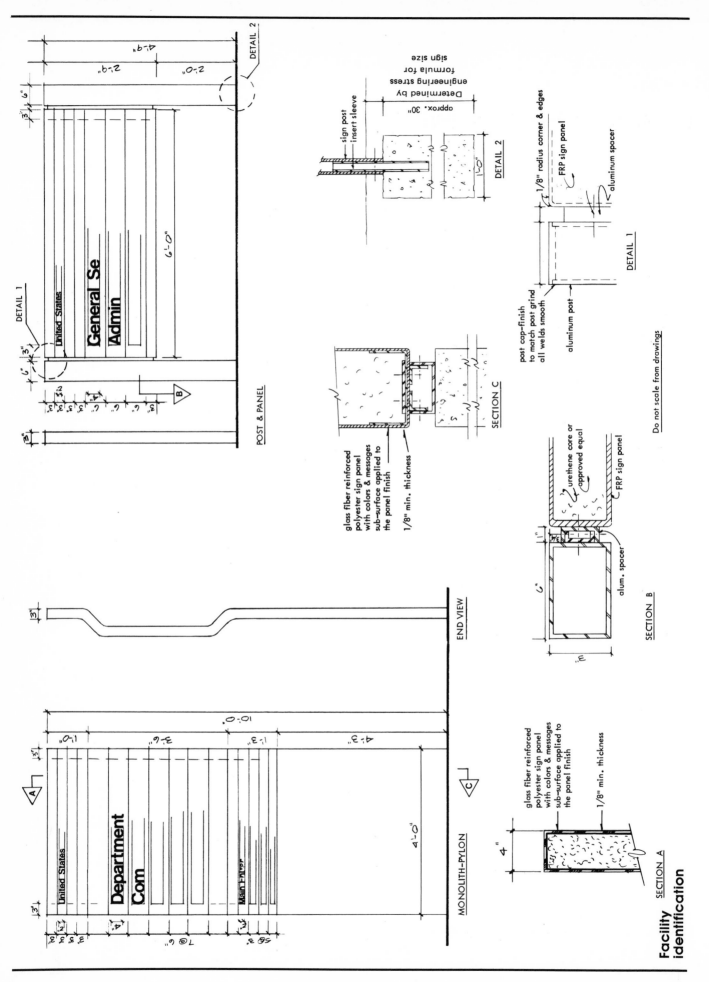

DETAIL 1

United States
General Se
Admin

6'-0"

4'-9"

2'-9"

2'-0"

3" 6"

3" 3"

6" 3"

B

POST & PANEL

DETAIL 2

Determined by
engineering stress
formula for
sign size

approx. 30"

sign post
insert sleeve

1'-0"

DETAIL 2

SECTION C

glass fiber reinforced
polyester sign panel
with colors & messages
sub-surface applied to
the panel finish

1/8" min. thickness

1/8" radius corner & edges

FRP sign panel

aluminum spacer

aluminum post

post cap-finish
to match post grind
all welds smooth

DETAIL 1

Do not scale from drawings

END VIEW

3"

urethene core or
approved equal

FRP sign panel

alum. spacer

6"

3"

SECTION B

MONOLITH-PYLON

C

United States
Department
Com

Main Entr

10'-0"

4'-0"

4'-3"

1'-3"

3'-6"

1'-0"

3"

A

glass fiber reinforced
polyester sign panel
with colors & messages
sub-surface applied to
the panel finish

1/8" min. thickness

4"

SECTION A

Facility
identification

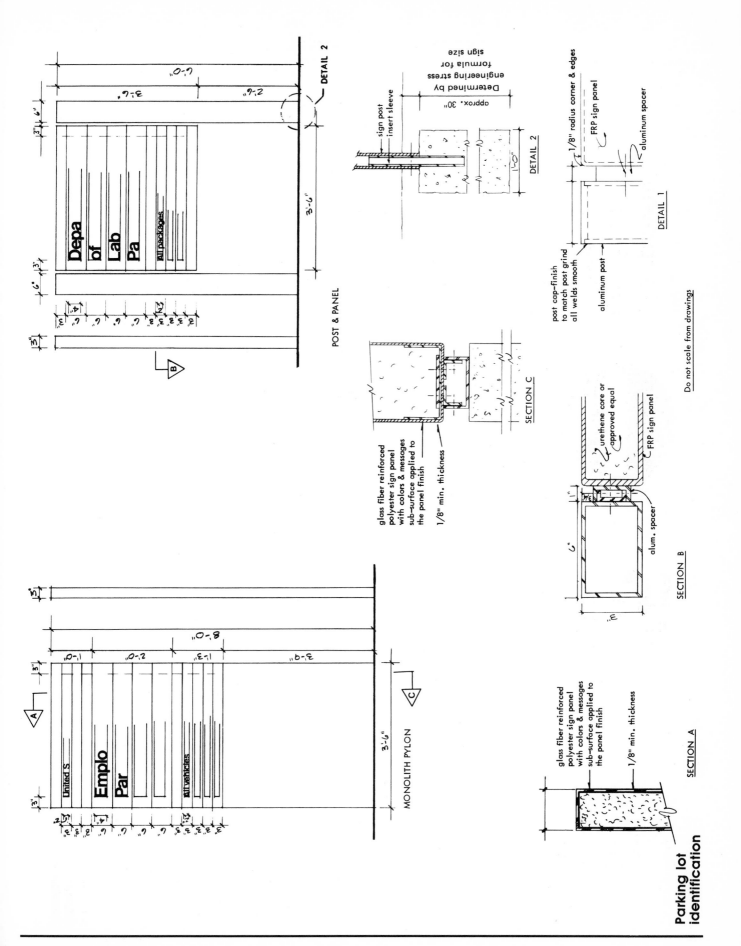

POST & PANEL

DETAIL 2

DETAIL 1

Determined by
engineering stress
formula for
sign size

sign post
insert sleeve

approx. 30"

1/8" radius corner & edges

FRP sign panel

aluminum spacer

post cap—finish
to match post grind
all welds smooth

aluminum post

Do not scale from drawings

SECTION C

glass fiber reinforced
polyester sign panel
with colors & messages
sub-surface applied to
the panel finish

1/8" min. thickness

urethene core or
approved equal

FRP sign panel

alum. spacer

SECTION B

MONOLITH PYLON

glass fiber reinforced
polyester sign panel
with colors & messages
sub-surface applied to
the panel finish

1/8" min. thickness

SECTION A

**Parking lot
identification**

Depa
of
Lab
Pa

all packages

United S
Emplo
Par

all vehicles

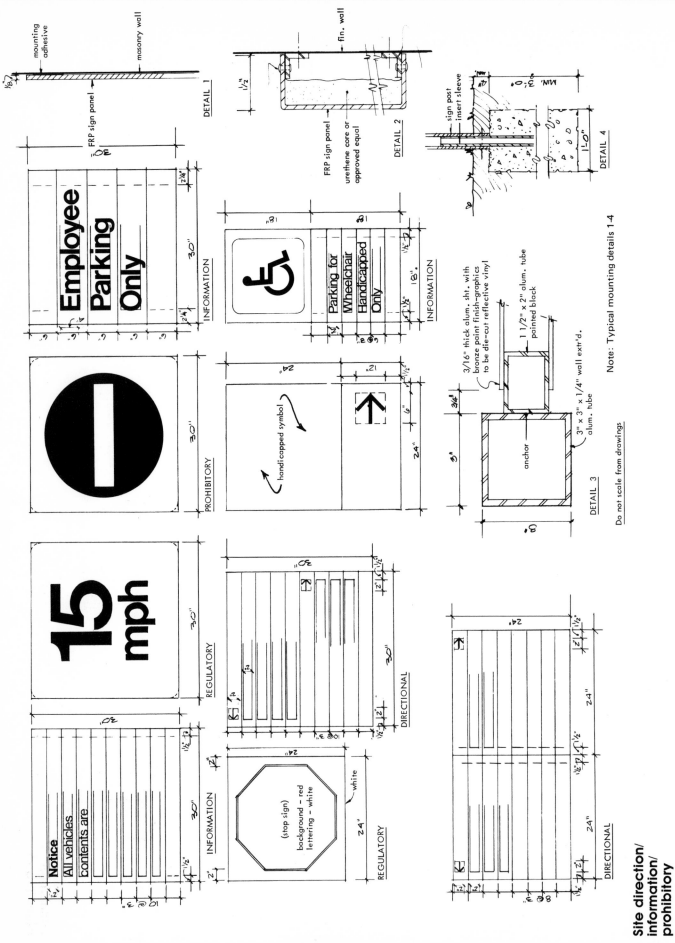

mounting adhesive

FRP sign panel

masonry wall

DETAIL 1

fin. wall

FRP sign panel

urethene core or approved equal

DETAIL 2

sign post insert sleeve

MIN. 3'-0"

1'-0"

DETAIL 4

Note: Typical mounting details 1-4

3/16" thick alum. sht. with bronze point finish-graphics to be die-cut reflective vinyl

1 1/2" x 2" alum. tube painted black

3" x 3" x 1/4" wall extr'd. alum. tube

anchor

DETAIL 3

Do not scale from drawings

30"

Employee Parking Only

2 1/4"

30"

2'

2"

2"

2"

3"

INFORMATION

18"

Parking for Wheelchair Handicapped Only

18"

1/2"

1/2"

2 @ 3

INFORMATION

30"

PROHIBITORY

24"

handicapped symbol

21"

6"

24"

1/2"

INFORMATION

30"

15 mph

30"

REGULATORY

30"

30"

DIRECTIONAL

1 1/2"

1 1/2"

2" 1 1/2"

2' 2'

1/2"

10 @ 3"

30"

Notice
All vehicles
Contents are

30"

1 1/2"

2'

1 1/2" 1 1/2"

10 @ 3"

INFORMATION

24"

(stop sign)

background – red
lettering – white

white

24"

2'

REGULATORY

24"

2 1/2" 2 1/2"

2' 1 1/2"

24"

1/2" 2' 2'

DIRECTIONAL

24"

2' 2'

24"

1/2" 2' 2'

8 @ 3"

DIRECTIONAL

**Site direction/
information/
prohibitory**

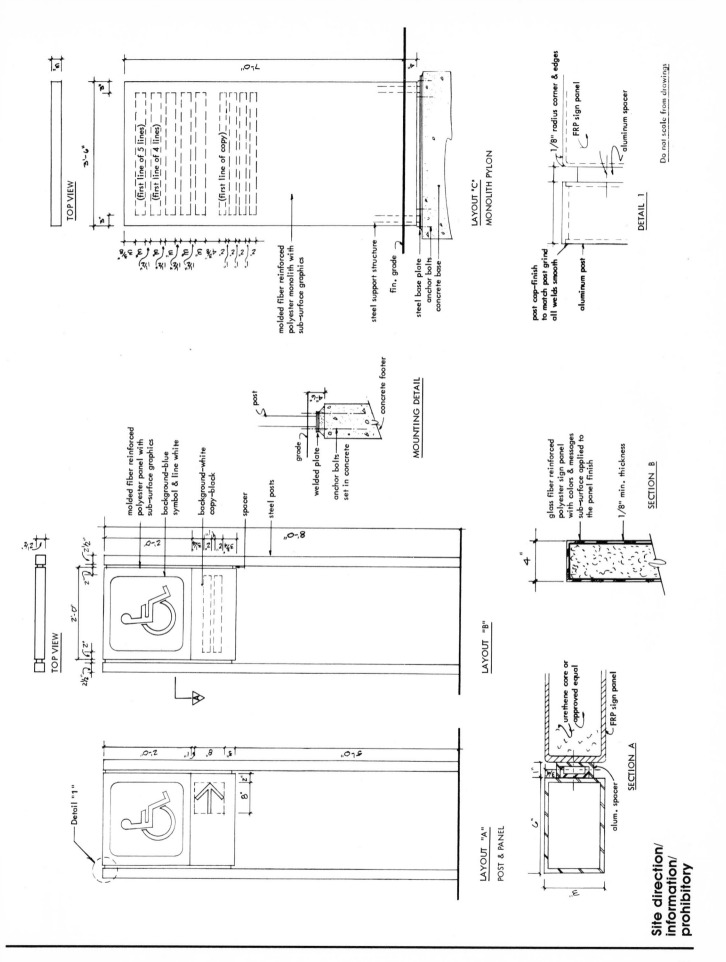

TOP VIEW

(first line of 5 lines)
(first line of 4 lines)

(first line of copy)

molded fiber reinforced
polyester monolith with
sub-surface graphics

steel support structure

fin. grade

steel base plate
anchor bolts
concrete base

LAYOUT "C"
MONOLITH PYLON

1/8" radius corner & edges

FRP sign panel

aluminum spacer

post cap-finish
to match post grind
all welds smooth

aluminum post

DETAIL 1

Do not scale from drawings

molded fiber reinforced
polyester panel with
sub-surface graphics

background-blue
symbol & line white

background-white
copy-black

spacer

steel posts

post

concrete footer

grade

welded plate

anchor bolts
set in concrete

MOUNTING DETAIL

glass fiber reinforced
polyester sign panel
with colors & messages
sub-surface applied to
the panel finish

1/8" min. thickness

SECTION B

TOP VIEW

LAYOUT "B"

Detail "1"

LAYOUT "A"
POST & PANEL

urethene core or
approved equal

FRP sign panel

alum. spacer

SECTION A

**Site direction/
information/
prohibitory**

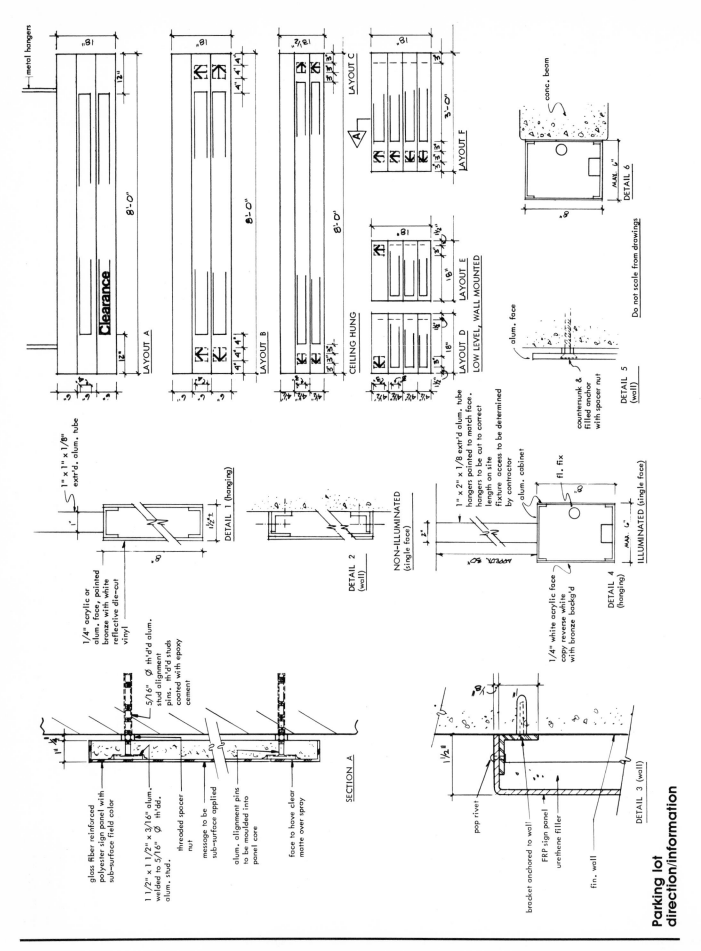

**Parking lot
direction/information**

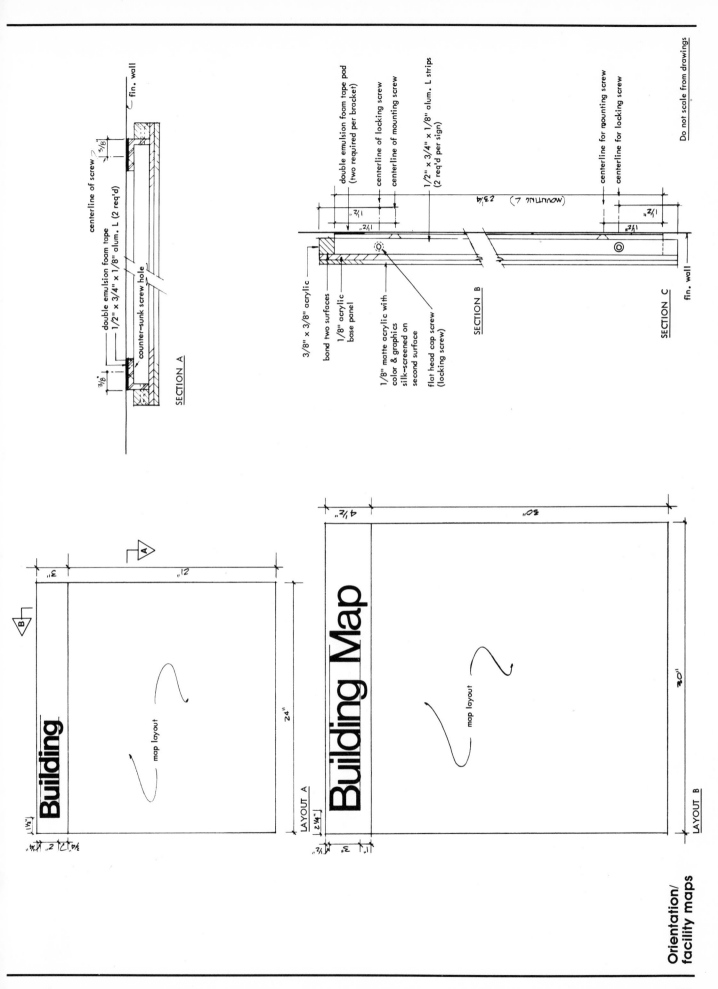

SECTION A

centerline of screw

double emulsion foam tape
1/2" x 3/4" x 1/8" alum. L (2 req'd)

counter-sunk screw hole

fin. wall

3/8"

5/8"

double emulsion foam tape pad
(two required per bracket)

centerline of locking screw

centerline of mounting screw

1/2" x 3/4" x 1/8" alum. L strips
(2 req'd per sign)

3/8" x 3/8" acrylic

bond two surfaces

1/8" acrylic
base panel

1/8" matte acrylic with
color & graphics
silk-screened on
second surface

flat head cap screw
(locking screw)

SECTION B

(MOUNTING L)

2 3/4"

centerline for mounting screw

centerline for locking screw

SECTION C

fin. wall

1/2"

1/2"

1/2"

1/2"

Building

map layout

LAYOUT A

3"

12"

24"

A

B

3/4" 2" 1/2"

1 1/4"

2 1/4"

Building Map

map layout

LAYOUT B

4 1/2"

30"

30"

1/2"

3"

1"

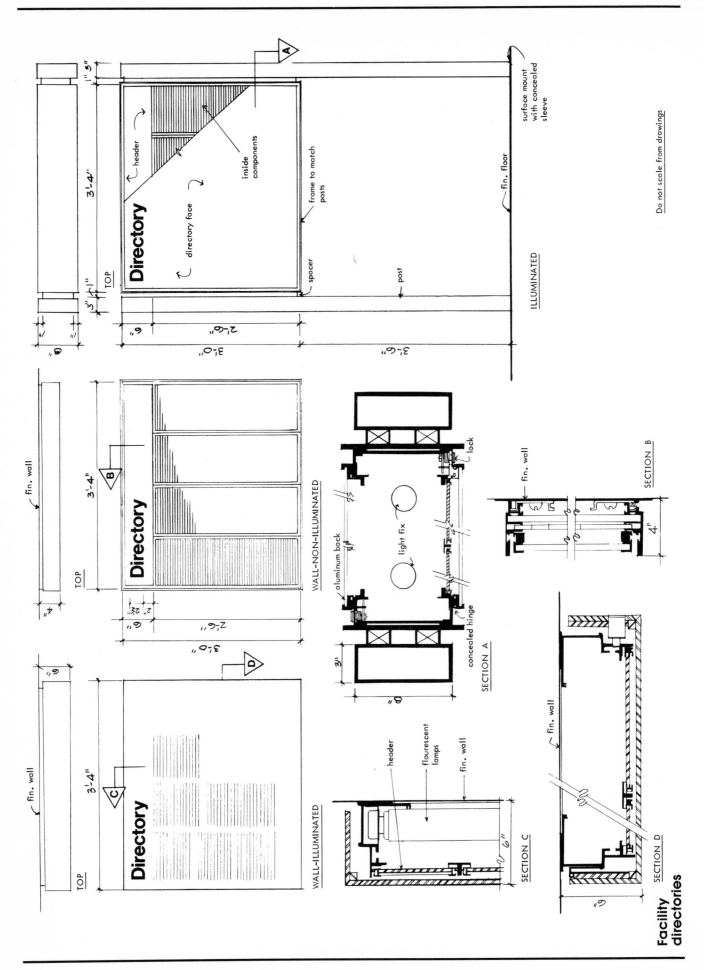

Do not scale from drawings

Directory

TOP

header

directory face

inside components

frame to match posts

spacer

post

ILLUMINATED

surface mount with concealed sleeve

fin. floor

3'-4"

1" 5"

3"

6"

2'-6"

3'-0"

3'-6"

---

fin. wall

Directory

TOP

B

4"

3'-4"

6"

2"

2½"

2'-6"

3'-0"

WALL–NON-ILLUMINATED

aluminum back

light fix

concealed hinge

lock

SECTION A

3"

6"

---

fin. wall

Directory

TOP

C

D

6"

3'-4"

header

flourescent lamps

fin. wall

6"

SECTION C

WALL-ILLUMINATED

---

fin. wall

SECTION B

4"

---

fin. wall

SECTION D

6"

Facility directories

104

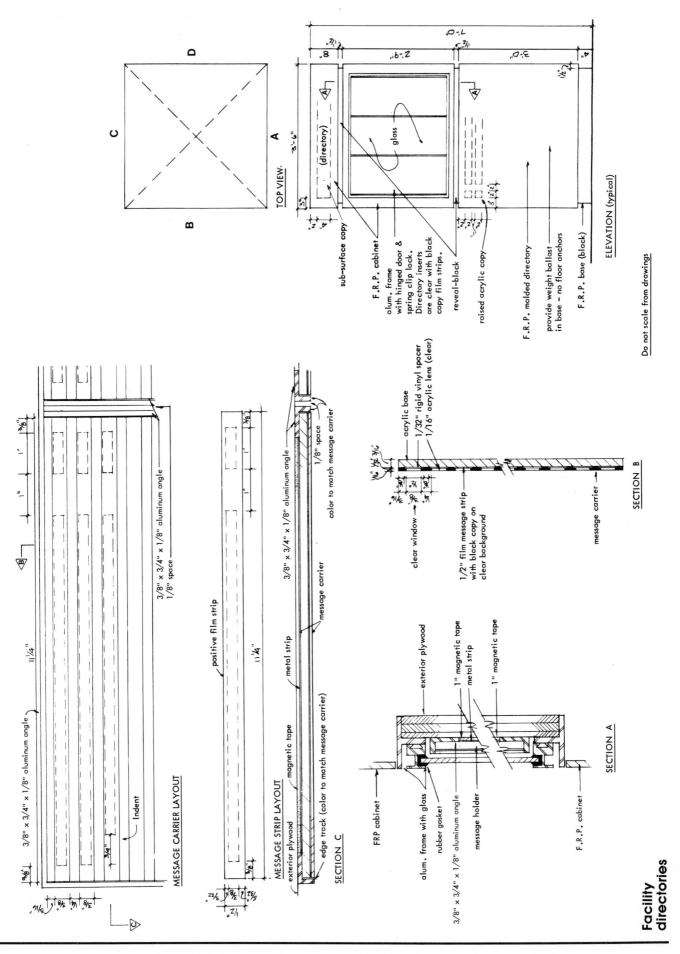

TOP VIEW

(directory)

glass

ELEVATION (typical)

sub-surface copy

F.R.P. cabinet
alum. frame
with hinged door &
spring clip lock.
Directory inserts
are clear with black
copy film strips.

reveal-black

raised acrylic copy

F.R.P. molded directory

provide weight ballast
in base – no floor anchors

F.R.P. base (black)

Do not scale from drawings

3/8" x 3/4" x 1/8" aluminum angle
1/8" space

MESSAGE CARRIER LAYOUT

3/8" x 3/4" x 1/8" aluminum angle

11¼"

Indent

positive film strip

magnetic tape

metal strip

message carrier

3/8" x 3/4" x 1/8" aluminum angle
color to match message carrier

edge track (color to match message carrier)

exterior plywood

MESSAGE STRIP LAYOUT

SECTION C

acrylic base

1/32" rigid vinyl spacer

1/16" acrylic lens (clear)

clear window

1/2" film message strip
with black copy on
clear background

message carrier

SECTION B

exterior plywood

1" magnetic tape

metal strip

1" magnetic tape

FRP cabinet

alum. frame with glass

rubber gasket

message holder

3/8" x 3/4" x 1/8" aluminum angle

F.R.P. cabinet

SECTION A

**Facility
directories**

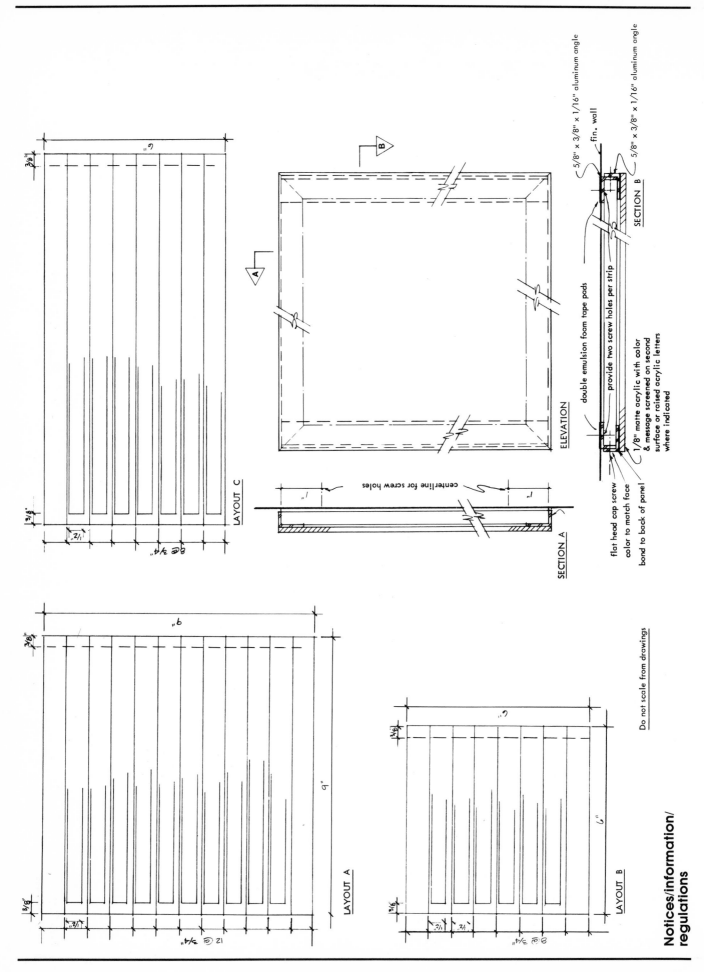

LAYOUT C

LAYOUT A

LAYOUT B

ELEVATION

SECTION A

SECTION B

centerline for screw holes

5/8" x 3/8" x 1/16" aluminum angle

fin. wall

5/8" x 3/8" x 1/16" aluminum angle

double emulsion foam tape pads

provide two screw holes per strip

1/8" matte acrylic with color
& message screened on second
surface or raised acrylic letters
where indicated

flat head cap screw
color to match face

bond to back of panel

Do not scale from drawings

**Notices/information/
regulations**

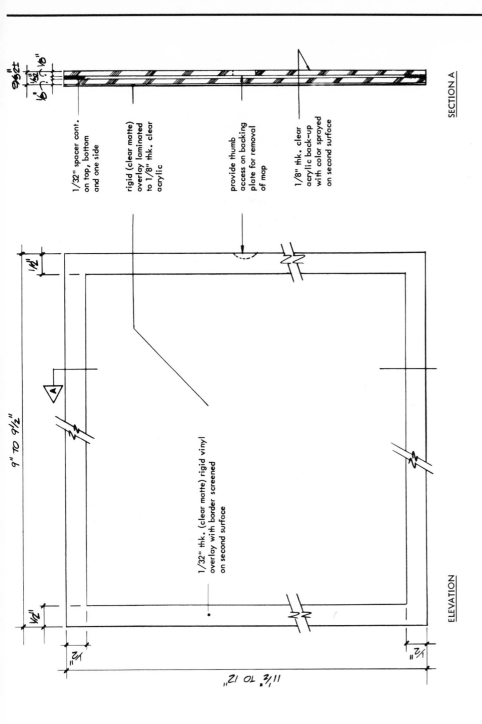

1/32" spacer cont. on top, bottom and one side

rigid (clear matte) overlay laminated to 1/8" thk. clear acrylic

provide thumb access on backing plate for removal of map

1/8" thk. clear acrylic back-up with color sprayed on second surface

SECTION A

2½"±

5/32"

1/8"

9" TO 9½"

½"

1/32" thk. (clear matte) rigid vinyl overlay with border screened on second surface

½"

½"

½"

11½" TO 12"

ELEVATION

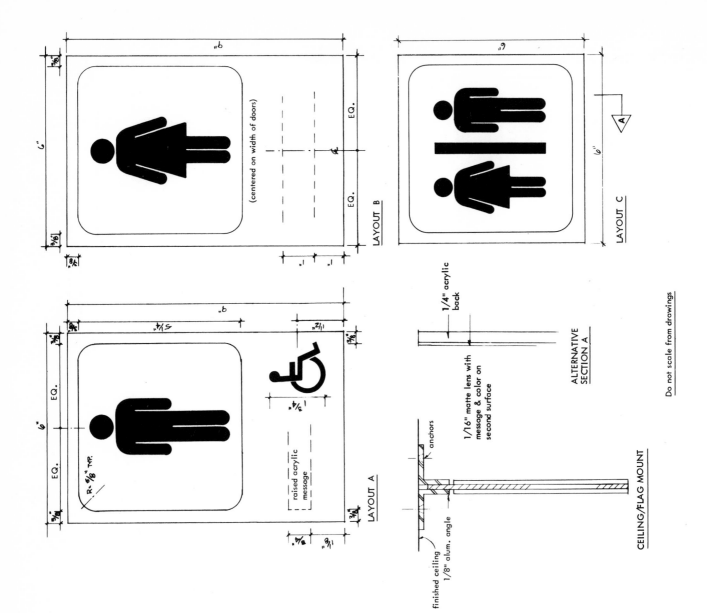

9"

6"

¾"

3⁄32"

3⁄32"

EQ.

EQ.

(centered on width of doors)

A

1"

1"

LAYOUT B

9"

6"

3⁄32"

3⁄32"

LAYOUT C

A

6"

9"

3⁄32"

3⁄32"

5¼"

EQ.

EQ.

6"

R- ⅝" TYP.

raised acrylic
message

1¼"

1¼"

1½"

⅝"

3⁄32"

1½"

LAYOUT A

¼" acrylic
back

1/16" matte lens with
message & color on
second surface

**ALTERNATIVE
SECTION A**

anchors

finished ceiling

1/8" alum. angle

CEILING/FLAG MOUNT

Do not scale from drawings

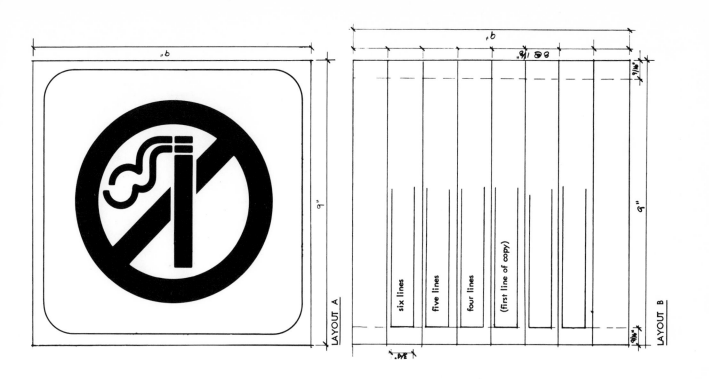

LAYOUT A

LAYOUT B

9"

9"

9"

9"

8 @ 1/8"

3/4"

9/16"

9/16"

six lines

five lines

four lines

(first line of copy)

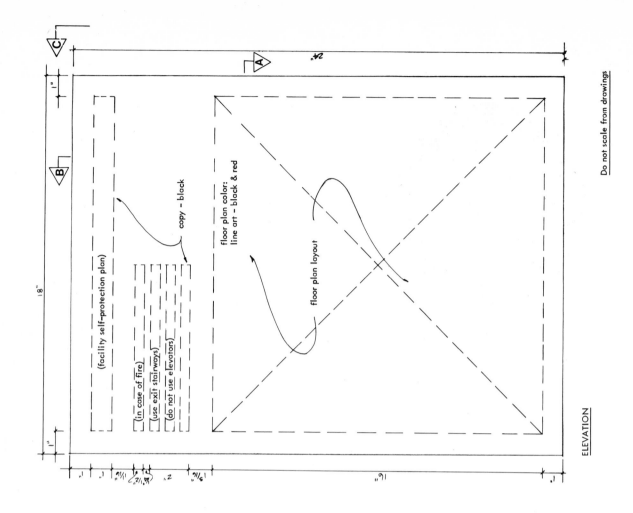

ELEVATION

Do not scale from drawings

(facility self-protection plan)

copy - black

(in case of fire)
(use exit stairways)
(do not use elevators)

floor plan color:
line art - black & red

floor plan layout

18"

1"

1"

24"

16"

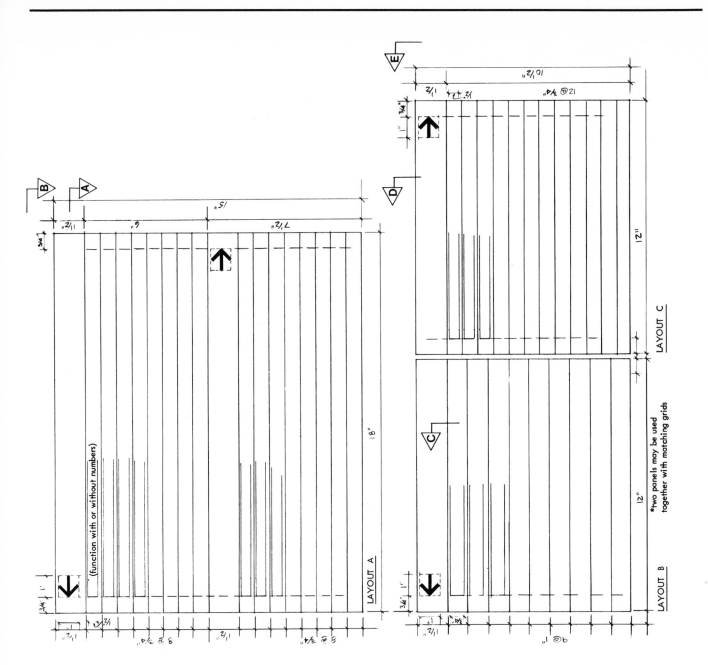

LAYOUT A

(function with or without numbers)

LAYOUT B

LAYOUT C

*two panels may be used
together with matching grids

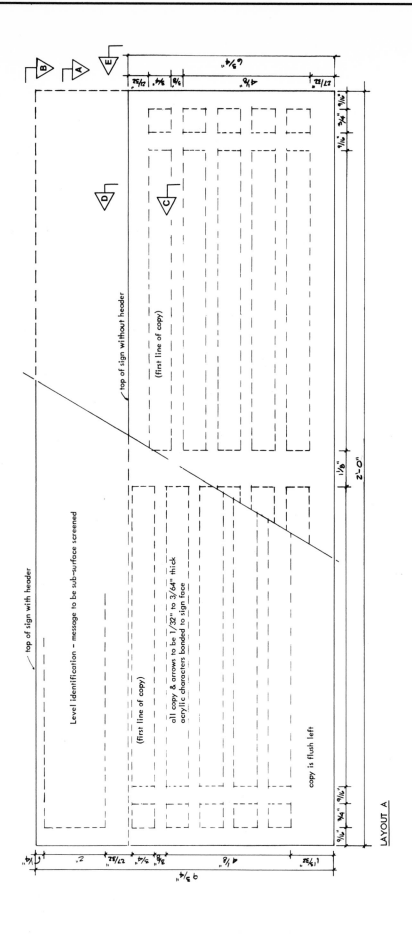

LAYOUT A

top of sign with header

Level identification – message to be sub-surface screened

(first line of copy)

all copy & arrows to be 1/32" to 3/64" thick
acrylic characters bonded to sign face

copy is flush left

top of sign without header

(first line of copy)

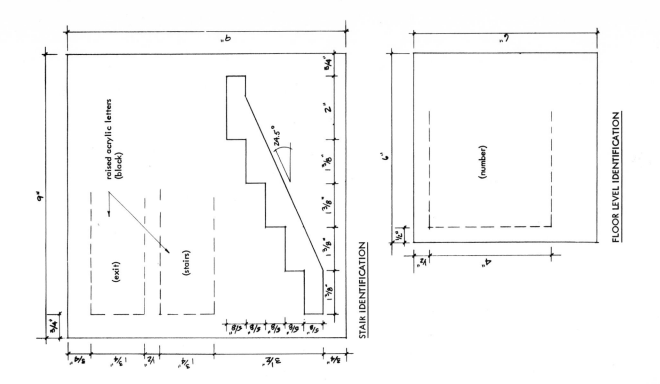

STAIR IDENTIFICATION

raised acrylic letters
(black)

(exit)

(stairs)

24.5°

9"

3/4"

3/4"
1 3/4"
1/2"
1 3/4"
3 1/2"
3/4"

5/8" 5/8" 5/8" 5/8" 5/8"

1 3/8" 3/8" 3/8" 1 3/8" 2" 3/4"

FLOOR LEVEL IDENTIFICATION

(number)

2"

6"

4"

1/2"

1/2"

**Floor and stair
identification**

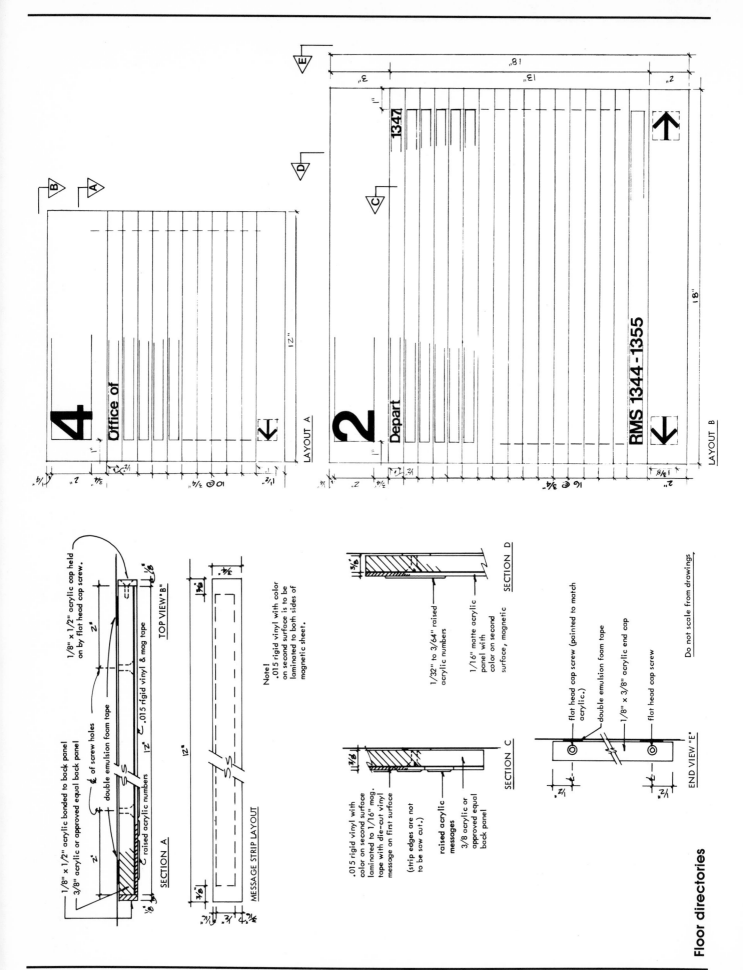

Floor directories

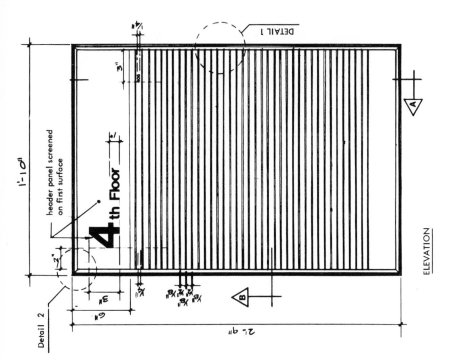

ELEVATION

header panel screened on first surface

4 th Floor

Detail 2

DETAIL 1

1'-0"

3"

2"

2'-9"

6"

3"

1/8" 1/4" 3/16"

A

B

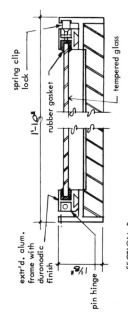

SECTION B

spring clip lock

tempered glass

rubber gasket

extr'd. alum. frame with duronodic finish

pin hinge

1'-1½"

1 15/16"

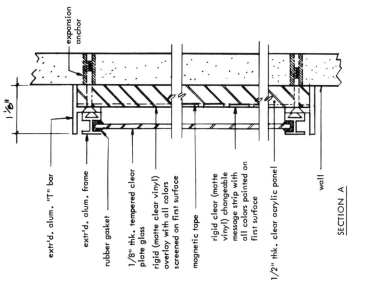

SECTION A

expansion anchor

extr'd. alum. "T" bar

extr'd. alum. frame

rubber gasket

1/8" thk. tempered clear plate glass

rigid (matte clear vinyl) overlay with all colors screened on first surface

magnetic tape

rigid clear (matte vinyl) changeable message strip with all colors pointed on first surface

1/2" thk. clear acrylic panel

wall

1 1/8"

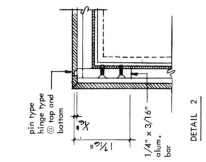

DETAIL 2

pin type hinge type @ top and bottom

1/4" × 3/16" alum. bar

1 7/16"

3/4"

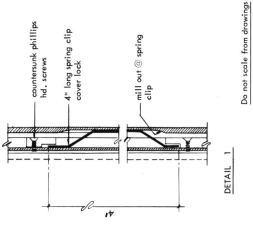

DETAIL 1

countersunk phillips hd. screws

4" long spring clip cover lock

mill out @ spring clip

4"

Do not scale from drawings

Floor directories

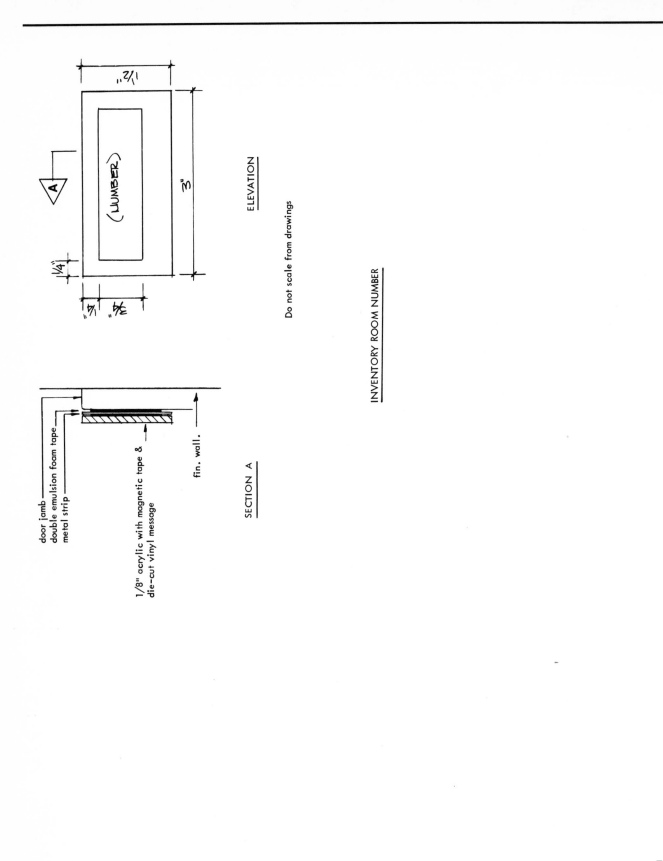

(NUMBER)

ELEVATION

1/2"

3"

1/4"

3/4"

Do not scale from drawings

INVENTORY ROOM NUMBER

door jamb
double emulsion foam tape
metal strip

1/8" acrylic with magnetic tape &
die-cut vinyl message

fin. wall.

SECTION A

**Inventory room
numbering**

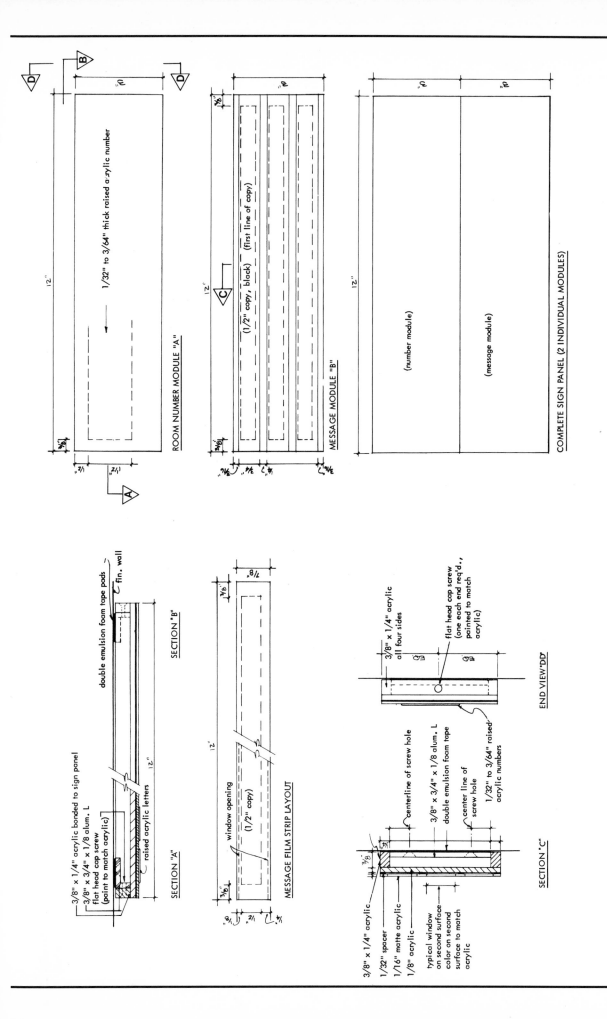

ROOM NUMBER MODULE "A"

1/32" to 3/64" thick raised acrylic number

MESSAGE MODULE "B"

(1/2" copy, black)   (first line of copy)

COMPLETE SIGN PANEL (2 INDIVIDUAL MODULES)

(number module)

(message module)

SECTION "B"

double emulsion foam tape pads

fin. wall

3/8" x 1/4" acrylic bonded to sign panel

3/8" x 3/4" x 1/8" alum. L

flat head cap screw
(paint to match acrylic)

raised acrylic letters

SECTION "A"

MESSAGE FILM STRIP LAYOUT

window opening

(1/2" copy)

END VIEW "DD"

3/8" x 1/4" acrylic
all four sides

flat head cap screw
(one each end req'd.,
painted to match
acrylic)

SECTION "C"

3/8" x 1/4" acrylic

1/32" spacer

1/16" matte acrylic

1/8" acrylic

typical window
on second surface
color on second
surface to match
acrylic

centerline of screw hole

3/8" x 3/4" x 1/8" alum. L

double emulsion foam tape

center line of
screw hole

1/32" to 3/64" raised
acrylic numbers

**Office
Identification**

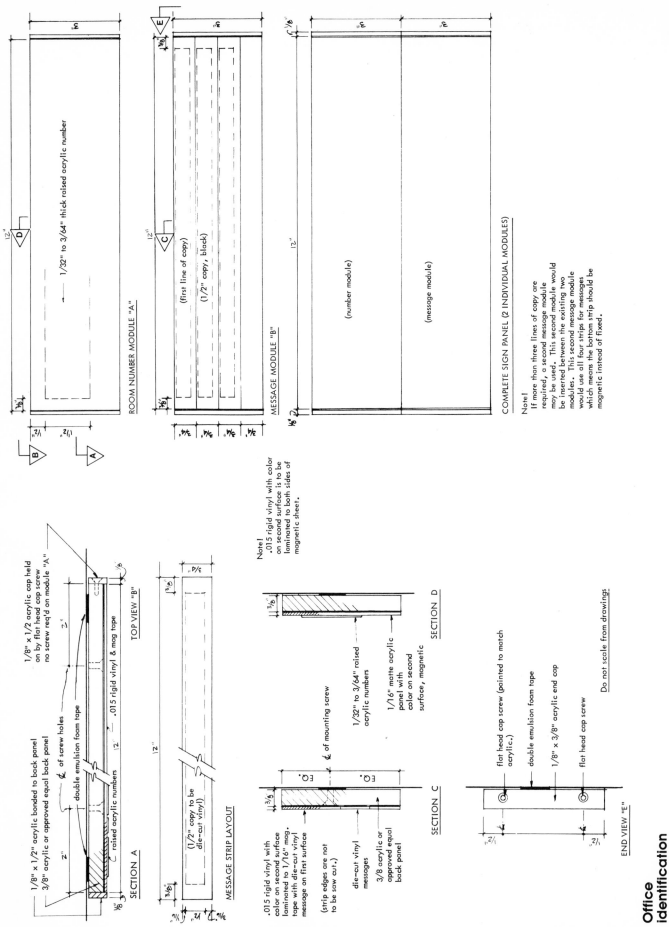

ROOM NUMBER MODULE "A"

1/32" to 3/64" thick raised acrylic number

MESSAGE MODULE "B"

(first line of copy)

(1/2" copy, black)

(number module)

(message module)

COMPLETE SIGN PANEL (2 INDIVIDUAL MODULES)

Note!
If more than three lines of copy are required, a second message module may be used. This second module would be inserted between the existing two modules. This second message module would use all four strips for messages which means the bottom strip should be magnetic instead of fixed.

SECTION A

1/8" x 1/2" acrylic bonded to back panel
3/8" acrylic or approved equal back panel

1/8" x 1/2 acrylic cap held on by flat head cap screw no screw req'd on module "A"

℄ of screw holes

double emulsion foam tape

.015 rigid vinyl & mag tape

raised acrylic numbers

TOP VIEW "B"

MESSAGE STRIP LAYOUT

(1/2" copy to be die-cut vinyl)

Note!
.015 rigid vinyl with color on second surface is to be laminated to both sides of magnetic sheet.

.015 rigid vinyl with color on second surface laminated to 1/16" mag. tape with die-cut vinyl message on first surface

(strip edges are not to be saw cut.)

die-cut vinyl messages

3/8 acrylic or approved equal back panel

SECTION C

℄ of mounting screw

1/32" to 3/64" raised acrylic numbers

1/16" matte acrylic panel with color on second surface, magnetic

SECTION D

flat head cap screw (painted to match acrylic.)

double emulsion foam tape

1/8" x 3/8" acrylic end cap

flat head cap screw

Do not scale from drawings

END VIEW "E"

Office identification

118

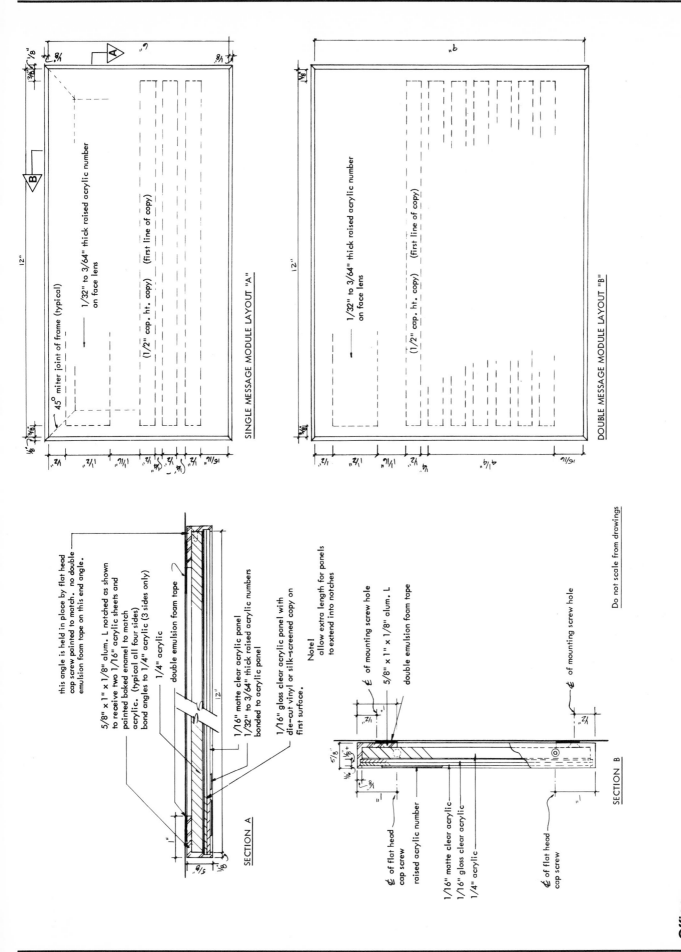

SINGLE MESSAGE MODULE LAYOUT "A"

DOUBLE MESSAGE MODULE LAYOUT "B"

1/32" to 3/64" thick raised acrylic number on face lens

(1/2" cap. ht. copy)

(first line of copy)

45° miter joint of frame (typical)

this angle is held in place by flat head cap screw painted to match. no double emulsion foam tape on this end angle.

5/8" x 1" x 1/8" alum. L notched as shown to receive two 1/16" acrylic sheets and painted baked enamel to match acrylic. (typical all four sides) bond angles to 1/4" acrylic (3 sides only)

1/4" acrylic

double emulsion foam tape

1/16" matte clear acrylic panel
1/32" to 3/64" thick raised acrylic numbers bonded to acrylic panel

1/16" gloss clear acrylic panel with die-cut vinyl or silk-screened copy on first surface.

SECTION A

Note!
allow extra length for panels to extend into notches

¢ of mounting screw hole

5/8" x 1" x 1/8" alum. L

double emulsion foam tape

¢ of mounting screw hole

¢ of flat head cap screw

raised acrylic number

1/16" matte clear acrylic
1/16" gloss clear acrylic
1/4" acrylic

¢ of flat head cap screw

SECTION B

Do not scale from drawings

Office identification

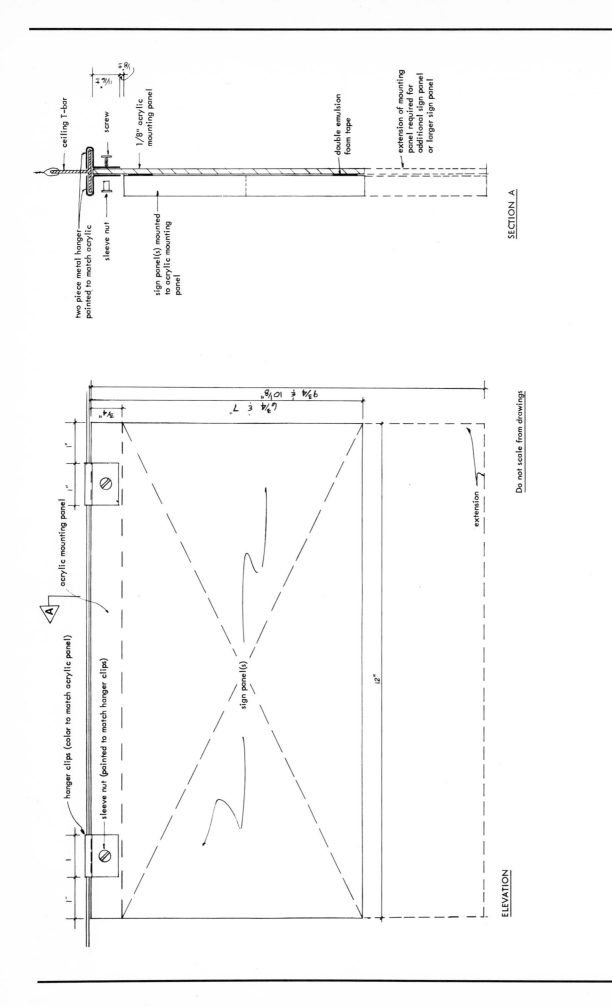

ceiling T-bar

screw

1/8" acrylic
mounting panel

$\frac{1}{8}$"±

$\frac{11}{16}$"±

two piece metal hanger
painted to match acrylic

sleeve nut

sign panel(s) mounted
to acrylic mounting
panel

double emulsion
foam tape

extension of mounting
panel required for
additional sign panel
or larger sign panel

SECTION A

acrylic mounting panel

$\overset{A}{\triangle}$

hanger clips (color to match acrylic panel)

sleeve nut (painted to match hanger clips)

$\frac{3}{4}$"

sign panel(s)

12"

$6\frac{3}{4}$" ± 7"

$9\frac{3}{4}$" ± $10\frac{1}{8}$"

extension

ELEVATION

Do not scale from drawings

**Ceiling mount
device**

120

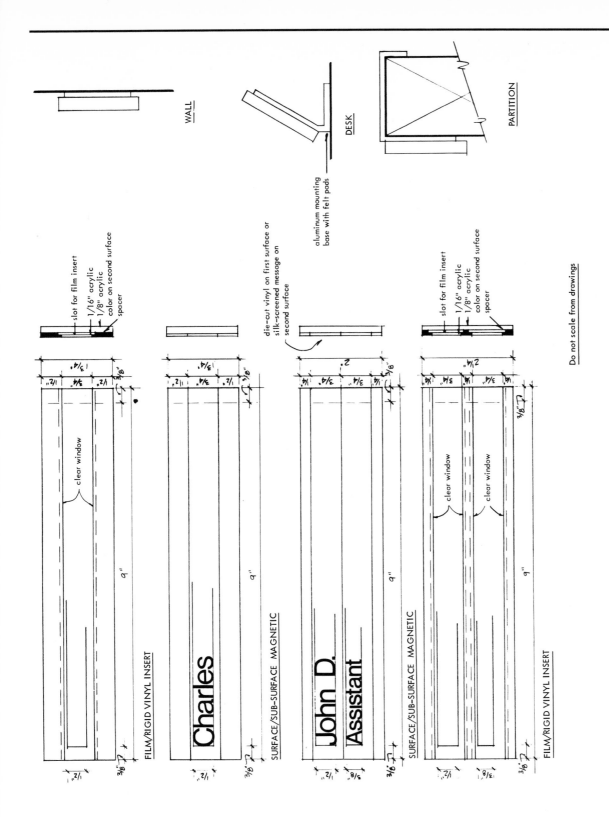

WALL

DESK

PARTITION

aluminium mounting
base with felt pads

slot for film insert
1/16" acrylic
1/8" acrylic
color on second surface
spacer

die-cut vinyl on first surface or
silk-screened message on
second surface

slot for film insert
1/16" acrylic
1/8" acrylic
color on second surface
spacer

Do not scale from drawings

clear window

FILM/RIGID VINYL INSERT

Charles

SURFACE/SUB-SURFACE MAGNETIC

John D.

Assistant

SURFACE/SUB-SURFACE MAGNETIC

clear window

clear window

FILM/RIGID VINYL INSERT

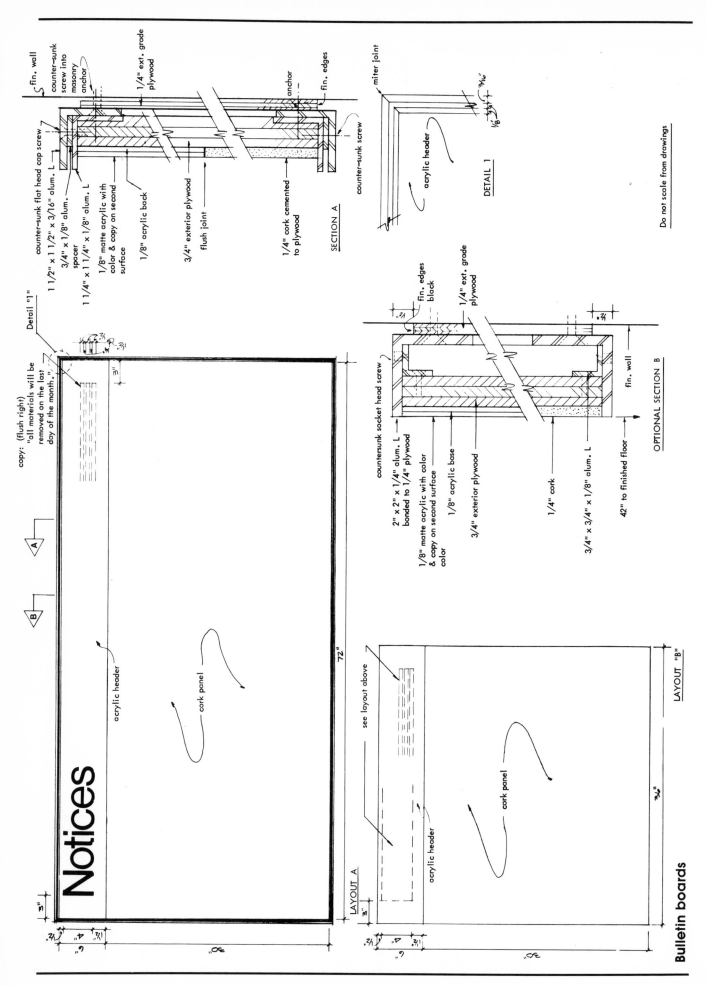

Notices

copy: (flush right)
"all materials will be removed on the last day of the month."

Detail "1"

1 1/2" x 1 1/2" x 3/16" alum. L
counter-sunk flat head cap screw
3/4" x 1/8" alum. spacer
1 1/4" x 1 1/4" x 1/8" alum. L
1/8" matte acrylic with color & copy on second surface
1/8" acrylic back
3/4" exterior plywood
flush joint
1/4" cork cemented to plywood

fin. wall
counter-sunk screw into masonry anchor
1/4" ext. grade plywood
fin. edges
anchor
counter-sunk screw

SECTION A

miter joint
acrylic header

DETAIL 1

Do not scale from drawings

acrylic header
cork panel
72"
3"
3"
30"
6"
4"
1 1/2"
1 1/2"

A
B

LAYOUT A

countersunk socket head screw
2" x 2" x 1/4" alum. L bonded to 1/4" plywood
1/8" matte acrylic with color & copy on second surface color
1/8" acrylic base
3/4" exterior plywood
1/4" cork
3/4" x 3/4" x 1/8" alum. L

fin. edges black
1/4" ext. grade plywood
fin. wall
42" to finished floor

OPTIONAL SECTION B

see layout above
acrylic header
cork panel
3"
3"
30"
6"
1 1/2"

LAYOUT "B"

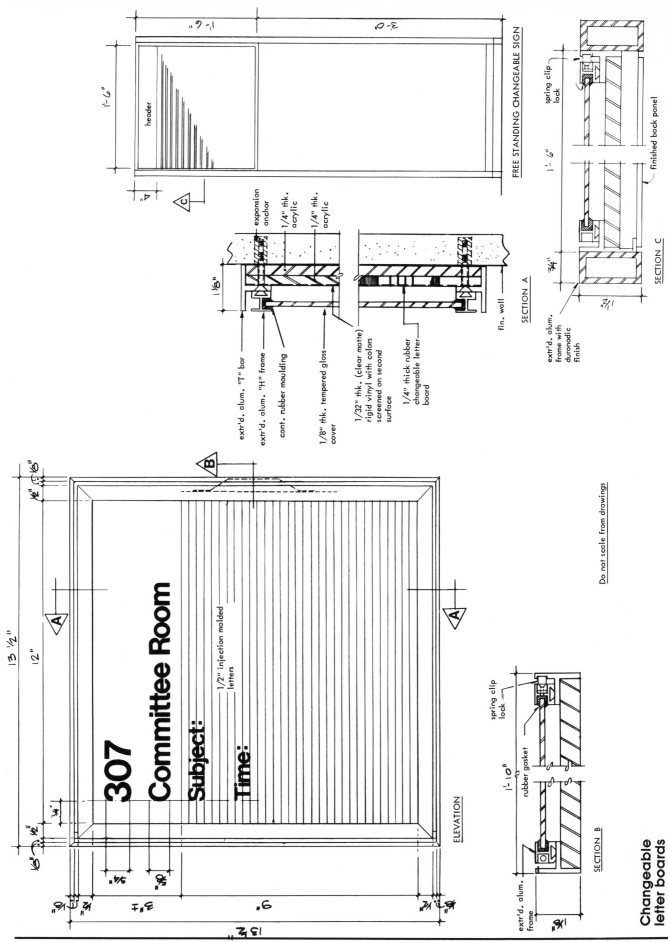

FREE STANDING CHANGEABLE SIGN

header

307

Committee Room

Subject:

Time:

1/2" injection molded letters

ELEVATION

13 ½"
12"

9"
3"±

expansion anchor

1/4" thk. acrylic

1/4" thk. acrylic

extr'd. alum. "T" bar

extr'd. alum. "H" frame

cont. rubber moulding

1/8" thk. tempered glass cover

1/32" thk. (clear matte) rigid vinyl with colors screened on second surface

1/4" thick rubber changeable letter board

fin. wall

SECTION A

spring clip lock

finished back panel

extr'd. alum. frame with duronodic finish

SECTION C

spring clip lock

rubber gasket

extr'd. alum. frame

SECTION B

Do not scale from drawings

**Changeable
letter boards**

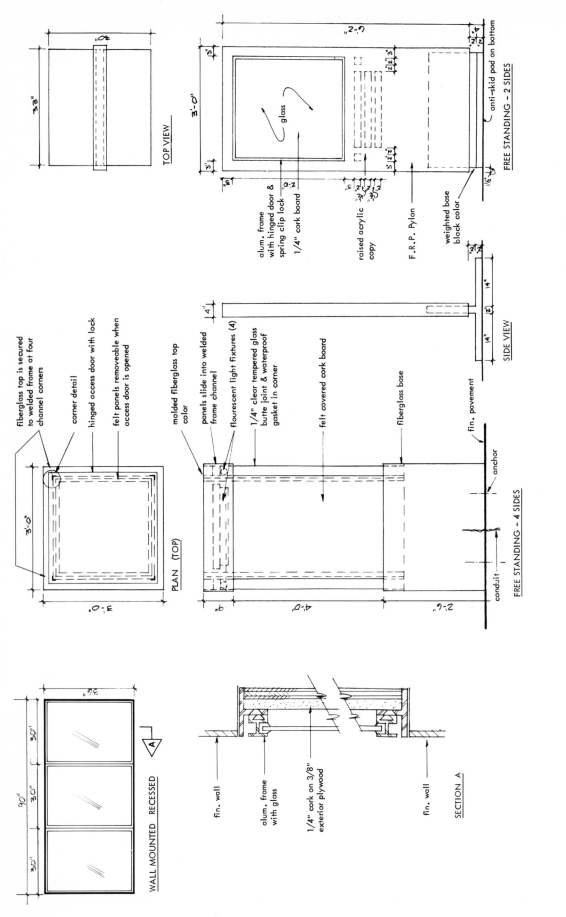

TOP VIEW

3'3"

3'-0"

glass

alum. frame
with hinged door &
spring clip lock

1/4" cork board

raised acrylic
copy

F.R.P. Pylon

weighted base
black color

anti-skid pad on bottom

FREE STANDING – 2 SIDES

Do not scale from drawings

PLAN (TOP)

3'-0"

3'-0"

fiberglass top is secured
to welded frame at four
channel corners

corner detail

hinged access door with lock

felt panels removeable when
access door is opened

molded fiberglass top
color

panels slide into welded
frame channel

flourescent light fixtures (4)

1/4" clear tempered glass
butte joint & waterproof
gasket in corner

felt covered cork board

fiberglass base

fin. pavement

anchor

conduit

FREE STANDING – 4 SIDES

SIDE VIEW

WALL MOUNTED RECESSED

A

9'0"

3'0"

3'0"

3'0"

3'6"

fin. wall

alum. frame
with glass

1/4" cork on 3/8"
exterior plywood

fin. wall

SECTION A

Display case

CHAPTER TEN

Technical Specifications

The following specifications reflect the minimum acceptable level of sign quality and performance. Optional specifications are provided to correspond to options illustrated in design intent drawings.

These specifications may be used as they are for project/contract documents, or they may serve only as a guide to the designer.

Exterior post and panel—embedded graphics
Exterior post and panel—subsurface graphics
Exterior monolith—subsurface graphics
Exterior post and panel—aluminum
Exterior wall sign
Cast metal letters
Parking sign, wall
Parking sign, hanging
Parking sign, illuminated
Building directories
Orientation/building maps and facility self-protection plan
Fixed message signs
Interior directional signs
Floor directories
Inventory room numbering
Office identification
Ceiling mount
Personnel identification
Bulletin boards
Changeable letter-board sign
Recessed display case
Die-cut vinyl on glass
Temporary message holder

EXTERIOR POST AND PANEL— EMBEDDED GRAPHICS

Sign panels shall be glass-fiber-reinforced polyester (FRP) material with color and messages embedded in the panel finish. Construction shall be of low-shrink thermosetting polyester resin not less than 30 percent by weight to conform with industry standards of the Society of Plastics, acrylic fortified with high solubility chopped strand glass mat. Ultraviolet inhibitors shall be added to the resin to produce the maximum in color stability. The sign panel material shall be nonstatic.

Panel Thickness: The thickness of the sign panel faces shall be $1/8$ in minimum consistently throughout.

This embedment is not achieved using gel coats or molding techniques but is a continuous process whereby the preprinted substrate is embedded into a resin with sufficient reinforcement to yield the required performance characteristics.

Sign Panel Edge Finish All edges of the panels shall be finished straight, square, and smooth with no evidence of finishing marks or color variation. All edges shall be colored to match the sign face with the same finish.

Sign Panel Back: In all cases, sign backs are to be finished to match the front face with or without copy or art.

Posts

1. Material—3-in-square aluminum tubing
2. Color—finish
3. Spacers—for single-face sign, use a $1^1/2$- x 2-in angle with the sign panel bonded onto the angle flange. For a two-sided sign, use a $1^1/2$- x 2-in rectangular tube, bonding sign panels to each side.

Optional Graphic Application

Material: All sign panels shall be glass-fiber-reinforced polyester (FRP) material with color embedded in the panel finish.

Graphic Application: Die-cut vinyl, pressure-sensitive legends, minimum 0.003 to 0.006 in maximum film thickness, 3M Company Scotchcal or approved equal.

Optional Mounting:: For single sign panels using 3-in-square tube for single-post mounting. Fastening may be with threaded bolts with shallow round head without slots, mounted through predrilled sign panel and post, fastened with lock washer and nut.

EXTERIOR POST AND PANEL— SUBSURFACE GRAPHICS

Sign panels shall be glass-fiber-reinforced polyester (FRP) material with color and messages subsurface applied to the panel finish. Construction shall be of low-shrink thermosetting polyester resin not less than 30 percent by weight to conform with industry standards of the Society of Plastics, acrylic-fortified with high-solubility chopped strand glass mat. Ultraviolet inhibitors shall be added to the resin to produce the maximum in color stability. The sign panel material shall be nonstatic.

Panel Thickness: The thickness of the sign panel faces, corners, and edges shall be $1/8$ in minimum consistently throughout.

The panel core should be encapsulated in 2-lb-minimum low-density polyurethene foam or approved equal, as an integral part of the panel. Corner reinforcement inside panels is required and shall be of 9- or 10-oz marine fiber cloth.

Sign Panel Edge Finish: All edges of the panels shall be seamless and finished straight, square, and smooth with no evidence of finishing marks or color variation. All edges shall be colored to match the sign face with the same finish. There shall be no rounded edges or corners for all signs except for minimum rounded edges caused by molding of exterior signs.

Sign Panel Back: In all cases, sign backs are to be finished to match the front face and edges with or without copy or art.

Color for this category of signs shall be as shown on the drawings.

Support posts and spacers shall be steel, or aluminum erected in a manner to withstand all actions imposed by use such as wind, water, and similar forces. Fabricate supports with ground-level anchors in foundations in undisturbed soil or to existing pavement. Anchors are to be located 4 to 6 in below finished grade for concealment in soil only.

Finish for posts, spacers, and panels shall be painted matte finish.

Provide smooth surface finish that is free from sags, runs, skips, lines, ridges, variations in color, orange peel, bubbles, pinholes, mottling, crazing, coarse particles, and grit.

Optional Graphic Application

Material: All sign panels shall be glass-fiber-reinforced polyester (FRP) material with color subsurface applied to the panel finish.

Graphic Application: Die-cut vinyl, pressure-sensitive legends, minimum 0.003 to 0.006 in maximum film thickness, 3M Company Scotchcal or approved equal.

Execute die-cutting in such a manner that all edges and corners of finished letterforms are true and clean. Letterforms with round positive or negative corners, nicked, cut, or ragged edges, etc., will not be acceptable.

Thickness: Maximum 0.003 in for nonreflectorized, maximum 0.007 in for reflectorized.

Adhesive Quality For die-cut vinyl or screened messages: minimum 55 oz per inch width, after curing for 24 hours, required to break adhesive bond.

Changeability: Capable of removal, without damage to surface on which applied, by means of suitable liquid remover solvent.

EXTERIOR MONOLITH—SUBSURFACE GRAPHICS

All sign monoliths shall be glass-fiber-reinforced polyester (FRP) material with color and messages subsurface applied to the panel finish. Construction shall be of low-shrink thermosetting polyester resin not less than 30 percent by weight to conform with industry standards of the Society of Plastics, acrylic-fortified with high solubility chopped strand glass mat. The panel faces must be integrally molded with seamless sides and must be totally enclosed with an allowable minimum radius of 1/8 in. Ultraviolet inhibitors shall be added to the resin to produce the maximum in color stability. The sign panel material shall be nonstatic.

Monoliths are to be flush-mounted to the ground (no mounting base revealed), erected in a manner to withstand all actions imposed by factors such as wind, water, and similar forces. Fabricate with ground-level anchors in concrete foundations in undisturbed soil. Anchors are to be located 4 to 6 in below finished grade for concealment in soil only.

Color for this category of signs shall be as indicated on the drawings.

These monoliths are nonilluminated.

Lettering and graphic messages are photographically silk-screened or by similar approved method onto the sign substrate or gel coat. A clear polyester or polyurethane nonglare, semigloss layer is then applied.

The panel core should be encapsulated in 2-lb-minimum low-density polyurethene foam or approved equal, as an integral part of the panel. Corner reinforcement inside panels is required and shall be of 9- or 10-oz marine fiber cloth.

1. The resins must include an ultraviolet inhibitor, and the resultant sheet shall be able to perform outdoors without surface spalling, fiber bloom, or other surface deterioration.

2. The thickness of the sign panel faces, corners, and edges shall be 1/8 in minimum consistently throughout.

EXTERIOR POST AND PANEL— ALUMINUM

Material: All sign panels shall be 3/16-in aluminum sheet material with color painted with polyurethane paint or its equivalent.

Graphic Application: Reflective die-cut vinyl, pressure-sensitive legends, minimum 0.003 to 0.006 in maximum film thickness, 3M Company Scotchcal or approved equal.

Sign Panel Back: In all cases, sign backs are to be finished to match the front face with or without copy or art.

Posts

1. Material—3-in-square aluminum tubing
2. Color—finish
3. Spacers—for single-face sign, use a 1½- x 2-in angle with the sign panel bonded onto the angle flange. For a two-sided sign, use a 1½- x 2-in rectangular tube, bonding sign panels to each side.

Posts must be removable within 4 to 6 in of

finished surface, when mounted in soil, by means of postsleeve or base-plate method.

Optional Material

Face shall be fabricated of 0.125-in-thick aluminum plate, and shall be mounted to aluminum channel with countersunk blind rivets located not more than 4 in O.C. around the entire perimeter. All holes shall be filled and ground smooth. Exterior surfaces shall be primed, and spray-processed with epoxy base paint. Copy shall be silk-screened with either urethane or epoxy ink.

EXTERIOR WALL SIGN

All sign panels shall be glass-fiber-reinforced polyester (FRP) material with color and messages subsurface applied to the panel finish. Construction shall be of low-shrink thermosetting polyester resin not less than 30 percent by weight to conform with industry standards of the Society of Plastics, acrylic fortified with high-solubility chopped strand glass mat. The panel faces must be integrally molded with seamless sides and must be totally enclosed with an allowable minimum radius of $1/8$ in. Ultraviolet inhibitors shall be added to the resin to produce the maximum in color stability. The sign panel material shall be nonstatic.

1. The resins must include an ultraviolet inhibitor, and the resultant sheet shall be able to perform outdoors without surface spalling, fiber bloom, or other surface deterioration.

2. The thickness of the sign panel faces, corners, and edges shall be $1/8$ in minimum consistently throughout.

Lettering and graphic messages are photographically silk-screened or by similar approved method onto the sign substrate or gel coat. A clear polyester or polyurethane nonglare, semigloss layer is them applied.

Mounting: Panel to mount to finished wall with aluminum angle bracket or shall be mounted flat to masonry wall with a combination of foam tape and silicone adhesive.

CAST METAL LETTERS

The items shall consist of cast aluminum letters in typeface using upper- and lowercase alphabets. The cap height size is as indicated on the drawings. Letter depth shall be according to manufacturer's specifications.

The finish shall be matte, baked enamel, or porcelain.

All edges shall be clear of mold or machine marks. The surface of the letter face shall be free of scratches, dirt, and pits.

Standard letter spacing shall be used. Spacing templates for installation are required. Exact spacing and layout for templates shall be resolved between the contractor and the architect on site.

The letters shall be flush-mounted with threaded noncorrosive studs held in cement. Extreme care must be taken in working with the concrete surfaces so as not to damage or disturb the finish.

PARKING SIGN, WALL

The sign type utilizes a single-sided panel with a 1-in integral molded return and encapsulated core.

The sign panels shall be glass-fiber-reinforced polyester (FRP) material with color and messages embedded in the panel finish. Construction shall be of low-shrink themosetting polyester resin not less than 30 percent by weight to conform with industry standards of the Society of Plastics, acrylic fortified with high solubility chopped strand glass mat. The panel faces must be integrally molded with returns. Ultraviolet inhibitors shall be added to the resin to produce the maximum in color stability. The sign panel material shall be nonstatic.

Panel Thickness: The thickness of the sign panel faces, corners, and edges shall be $1/8$ in minimum consistently throughout.

The panel back should be encapsulated in 2-lb-minimum low-density polyurethane foam or its approved equivalent, as an integral part of the panel. Corner reinforcement inside panels is required, and shall be of 9- or 10-oz marine fiber cloth.

Sign Panel Edge Finish: All edges of the panels shall be seamless and finished straight, square, and smooth with no evidence of finishing marks or color variation. All edges shall be colored to match the sign face with the same finish. There shall be no rounded edges or corners for all signs except for minimum rounded edges caused by molding of exterior signs.

Signs are to be mounted to walls using one of two methods:

1. Angle brackets are mounted to walls with appropriate anchors. The sign panels are then attached to the angle flanges through the top and bottom return of the sign.

2. Flat sign panels without returns may be mounted with double-sided foam or liquid adhesive such as silicone cement.

Optional Material

Angle brackets may be mounted to the aluminum face panel. The sign panel is then attached to angle brackets mounted to the concrete. Screws or pop rivets may be used.

Flat panels without angle returns may be mounted with anchor bolts countersunk, filled, and ground smooth. A spacer nut will be drawn snugly against the back of the panel. The exposed anchor pin will be set in masonry epoxy or cement.

PARKING SIGN, HANGING

All sign panels shall be glass-fiber-reinforced polyester (FRP) material with color and messages embedded in the panel finish. Construction shall be of low-shrink themosetting polyester resin not less than 30 percent by weight to conform with industry standards of the Society of Plastics, acrylic fortified with high solubility chopped strand glass mat. Ultraviolet inhibitors shall be added to the resin to produce the maximum in color stability. The sign panel material shall be nonstatic.

Panel Thickness: The thickness of the sign panel faces, corners, and edges shall be $1/8$ in minimum consistently throughout. Color and messages are to be silk-screened onto a sign carrier, then embedded into the fiber-reinforced polyester resin.

This embedment is not achieved using gel coats or molding techniques but is a continuous process whereby the preprinted substrate is embedded into a resin with sufficient reinforcement to yield the required performance characteristics.

The panel core should be encapsulated in 2-lb-minimum low-density polyurethane foam or its approved equivalent, as an integral part of the panel. Corner reinforcement inside panels is required, and shall be of 9- or 10-oz marine fiber cloth.

Sign Panel Edge Finish: All edges of the panels shall be seamless and finished straight, square, and smooth with no evidence of finishing marks or color variation. All edges shall be colored to match the sign face with the same finish.

Color for this category of signs shall be as indicated on the drawings.

Support and spacers shall be aluminum. Sign supports shall be attached to the underside of the concrete structure which covers the area of the sign location. Adjustments in the length of hangers shall be made on site. The hangers shall be attached to the concrete with appropriate masonry anchors. This method must be approved by the contracting officer to avoid interruption of waterproofing or mechanical or electrical elements.

Finish for supports, spacers, and panels shall be matte.

Provide smooth surface finish that is free from sags, runs, skips, lines, ridges, variations in color, orange peel, bubbles, pinholes, mottling, crazing, coarse particles, and grit.

PARKING SIGN, ILLUMINATED

Ceiling-Hung

This sign type utilizes a single-face, aluminum-constructed enclosure.

The edges and back shall be aluminum, painted. The face panel shall be $3/16$- to $1/4$-in white acrylic sheet with reversed white copy on colored background. Paint shall be an epoxy or polyurethane type with a matte finish.

Lighting shall be UL-approved, 120V, high-output fluorescent fixtures. Access to lighting shall be provided by the contractor.

All edges, corners, and surfaces shall be smooth and free of finish marks or rivet/screw filler marks.

Support shall be 1- x 2- x $1/8$-in aluminum tubing with ceiling anchors to withstand all actions imposed upon them, such as wind. Supports shall be matte finish to match sign enclosure.

Conduit shall be run through supports from ceiling pigtail location to sign enclosure. Contractor will be responsible for electrical connections.

Wall-Mounted

Construction is the same as for ceiling-hung signs.

Mounting will be to vertical face of concrete beam with appropriate masonry anchors. Access into sign enclosure for electrical wire must be made on site, since conduit pigtail locations are not centered on sign location.

Light fixture access shall be provided by the contractor.

BUILDING DIRECTORIES

Illuminated Directory

1. Size
2. Material—9 percent low-light-transmission bronze acrylic plastic face and sides, the cover being hinged for access.
3. Graphic application—photographic film negative or reverse silk-screened messages on clear plexiglass strips held in carriers to allow each message to be interchangeable.
4. Lighting—fluorescent lamps.
5. Headers—integral with film negative or strip carrier.
6. Mounting—directories may be surface-wall-mounted with approved dry-wall or masonry anchors or freestanding.

7. A security lock shall be provided for each directory unit.

No visible frame is to be used in forming the directory box.

Nonilluminated Directory

1. Size

2. Material—aluminum extrusion frame with clear Lexan or equal cover glass contained in the hinged frame with concealed lock.

3. Graphic application—silk-screened messages surface or subsurface applied onto acrylic message strips, held in place by magnetic strips or message carriers. The header is to be silk-screened to match the message strips.

4. Color—as indicated on the drawings.

5. Mounting—directories may be surface-wall-mounted with dry-wall or masonry anchors or freestanding.

Freestanding Directory Supports

Support posts shall be aluminum rectangular tube sections erected to finished floor surfaces with concealed sleeve mounts, bolted to the floor. Color as shown on the drawings. No exposed fasteners shall be visible through the support faces when attaching the directory box. If the directory is illuminated, provisions for concealed conduit and connectors shall be provided. Attachment of directory box to supports shall be determined by the contractor for approval.

BUILDING DIRECTORY, FREESTANDING MONOLITH

This unit is a monolithic molded glass fiber reinforced polyester unit with color and header subsurface applied. The directories are nonilluminated strip units incorporated into the monolithic structure. See exterior monolith and graphic application specifications for subsurface and die-cut vinyl.

The directory unit shall be as follows:

1. Material—acrylic message holders with black aluminum frame and glass doors.

2. Graphic application—photographic film positive messages held in carriers to allow each message to be interchangeable.

3. Headers—integral with the top of the monolith surface.

4. Mounting—monolithic directories shall be mounted with approved masonry anchors to concrete pavement with concealed devices.

5. A security lock shall be provided for each directory unit.

Machine-cut Acrylic Messages This item shall be $^1/_{32}$- to $^3/_{64}$-in acrylic sheet characters, machine-cut to

cap height as indicated on drawings. The edges of each character must be free from burrs, cut marks, and untrue edges. Characters shall be virgin color acrylic. Characters shall be bonded to FRP molded face with an epoxy type adhesive, with no visible excess of cement.

The message holders will be contained in an aluminum angle and T-section divider which are mounted to the plywood back panel. Magnetic tape strips are attached to the back of the holders and secured to matching metal strips mounted to the back panel.

ORIENTATION/BUILDING MAP AND FACILITY SELF-PROTECTION PLAN

This unit shall consist of a subsurface screen printed acrylic plaque face, bonded to an acrylic backing plate. The backing plate shall have a $^3/_8$- x $^3/_8$-in acrylic perimeter strip chemically welded to the reverse side.

Mounting: This unit shall mount to two vertical aluminum angles with countersunk flathead cap screws. Cap screw heads must be painted with a baked enamel finish to match acrylic.

Mounting angles may be mounted in initial installation with double emulsion foam tape. Provisions (countersunk holes) must be provided for alternate mounting.

Note: Final art for floor plans shall be provided to the contractor.

FIXED MESSAGE SIGN

This unit shall consist of a single $^1/_8$-in matte acrylic sheet with the message subsurface screen printed, or with raised acrylic letters as indicated.

Subsurface Screen Printed Message

1. Message—shall be silk screen printed on the reverse side of matte clear acrylic sheet, with background area spray-painted to match colors specified.

2. Silk-screen inks—shall be of material recommended by acrylic manufacturers for optimum adherence to acrylic surface.

3. Copy—shall be of phototypeset positives and shall be printed in such a manner as to produce a letter free from any rough edges or rounded corners.

Machine-cut Acrylic Messages This item shall be $^1/_{32}$- to $^3/_{64}$-in acrylic sheet characters, machine-cut to cap height as indicated on drawings. The edges of each character must be free from burrs, cut marks, and untrue edges. Characters shall be virgin colored acrylic. All characters will be upper-

and lowercase typeface. Characters shall be bonded to the face with acrylic type adhesive, with no visible excess of cement.

Message plate This shall be bonded to a continuous $^5/_8$- x $^3/_8$- x $^1/_{16}$-in aluminum angle frame. Frame to have mitered corners, and to be finished to match background color of message panel.

Mounting: This unit shall mount to two vertical aluminum angles with countersunk flathead cap screws. Cap screw heads must be painted with a baked enamel finish to match acrylic.

Mounting angles may be mounted in initial installation with double emulsion foam tape. Provisions (countersunk holes) must be provided for alternate mounting.

INTERIOR DIRECTIONAL SIGN

Unit shall consist of a combination of subsurface screen printed message and raised acrylic letters.

This unit shall consist of a subsurface screen printed acrylic plaque face bonded to an acrylic backing plate. The backing plate shall have a $^3/_8$- x $^3/_8$-in acrylic perimeter strip chemically welded to the reverse side.

1. Message—shall be silk screen printed on the reverse side of matte clear acrylic sheet, with background area spray-painted to match colors previously specified.

2. Silk-screen inks—shall be of material recommended by acrylic manufacturers for optimum adherence to acrylic surface.

3. Copy—shall be of phototypeset positives and shall be printed in such a manner as to produce a letter free from any rough edges or rounded corners.

Machine-cut Acrylic Messages This item shall be $^1/_{32}$- to $^3/_{64}$-in acrylic sheet characters, machine-cut to cap height as indicated on drawings. The edges of each character must be free from burrs, cut marks, and untrue edges. Characters shall be virgin colored acrylic. All characters shall be upper- and lowercase typeface. Characters shall be bonded to the face with acrylic-type adhesive, with no visible excess of cement.

If raised letters are not required, delete the above paragraph of the specification. All such requirements shall be determined at the local level when it can be established that compliance with requirements for the handicapped can be lawfully waived.

Mounting This unit shall mount to two vertical aluminum angles with countersunk flathead cap screws. Cap screw heads must be painted with a baked enamel finish to match acrylic.

Mounting angles may be mounted in initial installation with double emulsion foam tape. Provisions (countersunk holes) must be provided for alternate mounting.

FLOOR DIRECTORIES

Header and Bottom Module: Unit shall be of fabricated acrylic with magnetic face plate.

Face Plate: This shall be 0.015-in rigid vinyl with color on the second surface, laminated to $^1/_{16}$-in magnetic sheet. Message shall be raised acrylic number.

Machine-cut Acrylic Messages This item shall be $^1/_{32}$- to $^3/_{64}$-in acrylic sheet characters, machine-cut to cap height as indicated on drawings. The edges of each character must be free from burrs, cut marks, and untrue edges. Characters shall be virgin colored acrylic. All characters will be upper and lowercase typeface. Characters shall be bonded to the face with acrylic-type adhesive, with no visible excess of cement.

Message Holder This shall be fabricated acrylic, consisting of a backing plate of $^3/_8$-in acrylic or its approved equivalent with $^1/_8$- x $^1/_2$-in acrylic band, bonded to both vertical edges of unit. Backing plate shall have steel facing to accommodate magnetic face plate.

Mounting: Unit shall mount with two strips of double emulsion foam tape of initial installation. Countersunk mounting holes shall be provided in backing plate for alternate mounting.

Message Module: Unit shall be of fabricated acrylic, with removable magnetic message strips.

Message Strips: These shall be 0.015-in rigid vinyl with color applied to the second surface, laminated to both sides of $^1/_{16}$-in magnetic sheet. Message shall be prespaced die-cut vinyl. Message strips shall have machined smooth edges, shall be cut to mount flush to each other, and shall fit flush to top and bottom of backing plate. *Note:* Bottom (fourth) strip shall remain blank, and shall be permanently bonded to backing plate, to discourage unauthorized removal of message strips.

Message Strip Holder See above, except one side band shall be attached to base plate with flathead cap screw to facilitate removal of magnetic strips.

INVENTORY ROOM NUMBER

This unit shall be placed on upper right door frame of all rooms that do not have a standard room ID sign and number, i.e., rest rooms, storage, closets, etc.

Number Plate This shall be one-piece $1/8$- x $1 1/2$- x 3-in acrylic, with four-digit prespaced vinyl die-cut number. Plate shall have magnetic strips bonded to reverse surface.

Base Plate This shall be $1 1/2$- x 3-in steel plate with foam tape on one side, to mount to wood door frame.

OFFICE IDENTIFICATION FILMSTRIP

Unit shall be fabricated in a manner to allow a minimum of two modules (one number module and one message module) to form a complete room identification sign. If it is determined that more than three lines of copy are necessary to complete the message, one or more additional message modules may be installed flush with the bottom of the basic two-module unit.

Number Module: Unit shall be fabricated of acrylic, consisting of a $1/16$-in matte acrylic face plate, subsurface finished to match acrylic. Face plate shall be laminated to $1/32$-in rigid vinyl spacer, and then laminated to a $1/8$-in back plate. Message plate shall then be bonded to a continuous $1/4$- x $3/8$-in acrylic perimeter strip. Message shall be raised acrylic number.

Machine-cut Acrylic Messages This item shall be $1/32$- to $3/64$-in acrylic sheet characters, machine-cut to cap height as indicated on drawings. The edges of each character must be free from burrs, cut marks, and untrue edges. Characters shall be virgin colored acrylic. All characters shall be upper- and lowercase typeface. Characters shall be bonded to the face with acrylic-type adhesive, with no visible excess of cement.

Mounting: This unit shall mount to two vertical aluminum angles with countersunk flathead cap screws. Cap screw heads must be painted with a baked enamel finish to match acrylic.

Mounting angles may be mounted in initial installation with double emulsion foam tape. Provisions (countersunk holes) must be provided for alternate mounting.

Message Module: Unit shall be fabricated in the same manner as above with the exception that the $1/32$-in rigid spacer shall be manufactured as strips to mount horizontally as spacers to allow the use of filmstrip messages. Face plate shall be surface-finished to allow clear window areas to receive filmstrips. Spacers to be mounted parallel to horizontal, and at equal spacing.

Filmstrip Messages: Filmstrip positive shall be phototypeset black characters on a clear film base. Characters shall be upper- and lowercase. Characters shall be produced in such a manner that all edges and corners of finished letterforms are true and clean. Letterforms with round positive or negative corners, nicked, cut, or ragged edges, etc., shall not be acceptable. Film carrier base shall be of a clear rigid material that shall not sag or warp when inserted into message unit.

Mounting is the same as for the number module. Note that all modules must be fabricated in such a manner that when installed flush to each other, they produce an appearance of a single unit, with a minimum visible joint.

OFFICE IDENTIFICATION MAGNETIC STRIP

Unit shall be fabricated in a manner to allow a minimum of two modules (one number module and one message module) to form a complete room identification sign. If it is determined that more than three lines of copy are necessary to complete the message, one or more additional message modules may be installed flush with the bottom of the basic two-module unit.

Number Module: Unit shall be fabricated of acrylic, with magnetic face plate.

Face Plate: This shall be 0.015-in rigid vinyl with color on the second surface, laminated to $1/16$-in magnetic sheet. Message shall be raised acrylic number.

Machine-cut Acrylic Messages: This item shall be $1/32$- to $3/64$-in acrylic sheet characters, machine-cut to cap height as indicated on drawings. The edges of each character must be free from burrs, cut marks, and untrue edges. Characters shall be virgin colored acrylic. All characters shall be upper- and lowercase typeface. Characters shall be bonded to the face with acrylic-type adhesive, with no visible excess of cement.

Message Holder This shall be fabricated acrylic, consisting of backing plate of $3/8$-in acrylic or its approved equivalent, with $1/8$- x $1/2$-in acrylic band, bonded to both vertical edges of unit. Backing plate shall have steel facing to accommodate magnetic face plate.

Mounting: Unit shall mount with two strips of double emulsion foam tape on initial installation. Countersunk mounting holes shall be provided in backing plate for alternate mounting.

Message Module: Unit shall be fabricated acrylic, with removable magnetic message strips.

Message Strips: These shall be 0.015-in rigid vinyl with color applied to the second surface, laminated to both sides of $^1/_{16}$-in magnetic sheet. Message shall be prespaced die-cut vinyl. Message strips shall have machined smooth edges and shall be cut to mount flush to each other, and shall fit flush to top and bottom of backing plate. *Note:* Bottom (fourth) strip shall remain blank and shall be permanently bonded to backing plate to discourage unauthorized removal of message strips.

Mounting Strip Holder: See above, except one side band shall be attached to base plate with flathead cap screw to facilitate removal of magnetic strips.

Mounting: See above.

OFFICE IDENTIFICATION COMPONENT

This unit shall be fabricated to consist of a removable lens with a raised acrylic number and a removable message panel, contained within an aluminum angle frame.

Lens: Panel shall be $^1/_{16}$-in matte clear acrylic with raised acrylic number, cut precisely to slide into machined grooves in aluminum angle frame.

Message Panel: This shall be $^1/_{16}$-in gloss clear acrylic, cut precisely to slide into machined grooves in aluminum frame, behind clear lens.

Message: This shall be either prespaced die-cut vinyl or first surface silk-screened. Message to be black.

Message Holder This shall be fabricated, using $^1/_4$-in acrylic backing plate, with $^5/_8$- x 1- x $^1/_8$-in aluminum frame. Frame to be machined to accept two $^1/_{16}$-in acrylic sheets. Frame to be bonded to backing plate on three sides, with the remaining side to be attached with two flathead cap screws. Screws and aluminum shall be finished to match acrylic. The $^1/_4$-in acrylic sheet shall be drilled and tapped precisely to accept cap screws.

Mounting: Unit shall mount to wall with double emulsion foam tape to be placed on permanently bonded frame areas only.

CEILING MOUNT

This sign holder is intended to be used with any of the standard room ID signs.

Mounting Panel: This shall be a single piece of $^1/_8$-in acrylic, to which any of the previously specified ID sign types may be mounted. Sign panels to be

mounted to mounting panel with double emulsion foam tape.

Ceiling-Hung Mounting Bracket: Mounting brackets shall be incorporated which will clip onto the 1-in flange of the ceiling T-bar system. These clips shall be changeable to allow repositioning of the sign panel when required without difficulty and without damaging the ceiling T-bar system.

PERSONNEL IDENTIFICATION

The desk plaque consists of an acrylic back panel $^1/_4$ in thick with a $^1/_{32}$- to $^3/_{64}$-in-wide slot provided. The front face panel is $^1/_{16}$-in-thick P-95 matte plexiglass with color background silk-screened on the second surface.

This slot behind the face panel will accommodate changeable message strips. The copy is die-cut vinyl letters applied to the front surface of a 0.030-in-thick clear acrylic strip, or photo film positives may be used.

The base shall be anodized aluminum with an angled mounting surface.

The back panel shall be permanently bonded to the base. The edges of both back and front panels shall be smooth and polished. Felt pads shall be on both ends of the base.

Optional Method: The $^1/_4$-in acrylic back panel with $^1/_{16}$-in-deep slot cut the length of plaque to receive a $^1/_{16}$-in-thick message strip with color on second surface and message on first or second surface by silk-screened or die-cut vinyl. Message strip is held in place by magnetic tape and a metal strip.

BULLETIN BOARDS

This unit is a combination aluminum frame, with subsurface copy on matte acrylic, and $^1/_4$-in cork board laminated to a $^3/_4$-in exterior-type plywood base.

Subsurface Screen Printed Message

1. Message—shall be silk screen printed on the reverse side of matte clear acrylic sheet, with background area spray-painted to match colors previously specified.
2. Silk-screen inks—shall be of material recommended by acrylic manufacturers for optimum adherence to acrylic surface.
3. Copy—shall be of phototypeset positives and shall be printed in such a manner as to produce a letter free from any rough edges or rounded corners.

Aluminum Frames

1. Affixed frame—shall be $1\frac{1}{2}$- x $1\frac{1}{2}$- x $\frac{3}{16}$-in aluminum angle anodized. Corners shall be miter cut and deburred. Frame to be mounted to $\frac{1}{4}$-in exterior plywood and permanently affixed to wall with countersunk screws.

2. Floating frame—shall be $1\frac{1}{4}$- x $1\frac{1}{4}$- x $\frac{1}{8}$-in aluminum angle anodized. Frame to receive header plate and tack-board panels. Frame to be secured into affixed frame with countersunk flathead cap screws. Contractor to furnish two key-type wrenches to remove cap screws.

CHANGEABLE LETTER BOARD

This item is to be a standard changeable letter board. The frame is aluminum extrusion with a continuous hinged glass access door. The changeable letter board is to be slotted felt. White injection-molded letters, in one size of $\frac{1}{2}$-in cap height, upper- and lowercase. Sufficient fonts of both sizes should be included. There should be a concealed latch for locking. Helvetica Medium typeface is suggested.

An integral header panel for room number and identification shall be provided. This shall be acrylic sheet with the copy silk-screened on the second surface. Copy shall be white and the background shall be medium bronze.

Mounting shall be with screw mounts secured in wall anchors.

This unit may be freestanding with two inverted T vertical supports. The sign box shall be mounted between the two posts.

DISPLAY CASE

These units are monolithic molded glass-fiber-reinforced polyester units with color subsurface applied. All four sides provide recessed display areas with clear tempered glass enclosure.

1. Refer to exterior monolith specifications.
2. The display panels shall be $\frac{1}{2}$-in cork mounted to a rigid backing with bronze-colored felt fabric covering wrapped and secured in a manner to allow ease of fabric replacement. These panels shall be removable by access from the top of the display case through a removable hatch. Each of four panels shall be individually held in a track frame allowing ease of removal.
3. The glass case enclosure shall have no visible frames. Glass shall butt joint with continuous seal.
4. All joints and seams of the display case shall be weatherproof from rain and moisture.

5. Each side of the display unit shall be illuminated with fluorescent tubes concealed in a soffit at the top of the unit.
6. A security lock shall be provided for the access hatch at the top.
7. The color of the case shall be as specified on design intent drawing.

Display Pylon

This is a monolithic molded glass-fiber-reinforced polyester unit, with color subsurface applied. The unit is nonilluminated. See exterior monolith specifications.

Tack Board: This unit shall be $\frac{1}{4}$-in tan cork laminated to $\frac{3}{8}$-in exterior grade plywood. Tack-board surface shall be face and edge adhered to $\frac{1}{8}$-in aluminum T bar, as indicated on drawings.

Glass Door: Door shall be $\frac{1}{8}$-in glass, with anodized aluminum frame and shall hinge from one side. Door shall be secured with a spring-clip-type lock.

Base: Base shall be fabricated of 0.125-in aluminum, Heliarc welded. All edges ground smooth and anodized. Base shall be weighted.

RECESSED DISPLAY CASE

This unit utilizes an extruded aluminum frame with bronze anodized finish. The frame depth is $3\frac{1}{2}$ in with a $\frac{1}{8}$-in-wide face reveal on the front. The hinged door is surrounded by a $\frac{7}{8}$-in-wide frame which forms the front of the case. Tempered glass will be used in the door. Cylinder locks will be provided.

This unit will be recessed into the wall area with appropriate wood framing required to secure the case in place. The case frame should provide a projection on all four sides sufficient to conceal any irregularities in the wall opening.

Genuine, self-sealing tan cork background will be used, $\frac{1}{4}$ in thick bonded to $\frac{1}{2}$-in exterior-grade plywood.

Internal, concealed fluorescent light will be used with UL-approved fixtures and hardward.

Optional Header Panel

A matte-finished acrylic header may be provided with subsurface silk-screened message or die-cut vinyl letters applied.

The exact height and location for mounting should be determined on site by the designer.

DIE-CUT VINYL ON GLASS

Graphic application die-cut vinyl, pressure-sensitive legends, minimum 0.003 to 0.006 in maximum film thickness, 3M Company Scotchcal or its approved equivalent. These messages should be applied to the surface of the glass.

Execute die-cutting in such a manner that all edges and corners of finished letterforms are true and clean. Letterforms with round positive or negative corners, nicked, cut, or ragged edges, etc., will not be acceptable.

Reflectivity and Specular Gloss

1. Nonreflectorized messages—60° specular gloss of 35 to 45 units when measured in accordance with ASTM Test D523

2. Reflectorized messages—to meet quality standard of Scotchlite Brand Reflective Sheeting, Series 3270, engineer grade.

Thickness: Maximum 0.003 in for nonreflectorized, maximum 0.007 in for reflectorized.

Adhesive Quality: For die-cut vinyl or screened messages, minimum 55 oz per inch width, after curing for 24 hours, required to break adhesive bond.

Shrinkage: Maximum 0.10 percent, when measured after cooling to 70° F following subjection to 150° F for 48 hours, in mounted condition on each specified surface.

Tensile Strength: 2000 psi, minimum.

Tensile Elongation: 25 percent, minimum.

Tear Strength 0.15 lb per 0.001-in thickness.

Changeability: Capable of removal, without damage to surfaces on which applied, by means of suitable liquid remover solvent.

TEMPORARY MESSAGE HOLDER

This unit will hold an 8- x 10 1/2- or 8 1/2- x 11-in sheet of paper. Construction consists of a 1/8-in clear acrylic backup sheet with color applied to the second surface. Then a 1/32-in spacer on three sides is placed between the backup sheet on another 1/8-in clear acrylic sheet. Finally, a 1/32-in-thick matte acrylic or rigid vinyl overlay will be laminated onto the face of the front 1/8-in acrylic sheet. A 1/2-in border of color will be applied to the second surface of the 1/32-in overlay.

1. A recessed thumb access on the right edge should be provided for removal of paper insert.

2. The mounting will be with double adhesive foam tape or silicone adhesive.

PART FOUR

Appendix

A teacher who hesitates to repeat shrinks from his most important duty, and a learner who dislikes to hear the same thing twice over lacks his most essential acquisition. —William Gowers

Digest of the Data Base

This section refers specifically to the evaluation of the Federal Signage Demonstration Program.

In order to establish a sound and thorough basis for understanding the requirements of all federal facilities, data in the form of 59 questions categorized into 15 specific pertinent points and answerable with a "yes" or "no" was gathered at each of the sites visited.

THE EVALUATION QUESTIONNAIRE

Project: (name of facility)
Location/region: (GSA)
GSA building manager: (name)
Tenant representative: (name)
Designer: (name)
Fabricator: (name)

Question categories:
1. Relevant criteria
2. Economic soundness
3. Compliance with special requirements
4. Flexibility
5. Durability
6. Antivandalism
7. Replacement
8. Repairability
9. Fabricator adaptability
10. Security
11. Color
12. Lighting
13. Mounting
14. Size
15. Sign message information
16. Evaluation

The general assessments, derived from evaluation of the data collected, reflect the objective opinions of the consultant.

---

1. J. Edgar Hoover FBI Building
Washington, D.C./Region 3

Actual Evaluation: Due to the high level of security required for this building and the controlled, limited public access, minimal signage is required. The complexity of the building's plan eliminates standard use of directional signs. Color-coded corridor header signs direct movement and identify various corridors. Room identifications are coded to floor, wing, corridor, and room number. Directories are not a factor.

The internally illuminated exterior signs do not read well due to effect of ambient light. Film negative process does not work well outside.

The system does not address "special condition" signs. As a result there are many typestyle and material variations in evidence. Lack of easy access to replacement or change or additions is a factor in reducing total system continuity.

This system uses subsurface silk-screened and die-cut vinyl graphic applications on acrylic materials. These applications seem adequate and appropriate for their use.

Building management and the tenant seem generally satisfied with the basic system. The system, as it is, provides the minimum of needed information. The nature of the tenant use does not demand more. Replacement and service are potential problems for building management.

---

2. Columbia Plaza
Washington, D.C./Region 3

Actual Evaluation: This project suffers from two key problems: There was a lack of coordination between GSA and the tenant concerning tenant needs, and lack of proper follow-through in implementing the complete system. Many signs are incomplete; as a result, the old sign system is still in use. There are situations where the new signs provide part of the needed information, and the old system provides the rest.

There is a general lack of continuity in those elements of the system which are implemented. This may stem from items being provided by those people not familiar with the intended system.

Replacement items must be obtained from outside sources, which dilutes the motivation to adhere to the intended system design.

This system must be considered a failure, not from design and/or fabrication, but from less than desirable coordination and understanding between GSA and the tenant.

3. HEW South Portal
Washington, D.C./Region 3

Actual Evaluation: The major problem with this project is that it is incomplete due to lack of proper funding and coordination follow-through. While the system generally follows HEW's graphics manual guidelines, the lack of completeness detracts from the system's success.

None of the room identification signs have inserts provided. As a result, every conceivable method possible is used to add needed information.

As a special note, the exterior building identification is completely obscure.

The color code system does not work if for no other reason than a lack of use instruction. Lack of completeness of the system also lends to this problem.

This project completely falls apart simply due to its incompleteness and lack of follow-through coordination. The design and fabrication are acceptable. However, replacement is based on outside sources and will be a hindrance.

4. Federal Triangle
Washington, D.C./Region 3

Actual Evaluation: The design of this system and the signs is quite acceptable. The existing fabrication is questionable. There are a number of bubbles and cracks in the finish. The layout in one instance does not accommodate the message length properly. The fabricator should have informed the designer for adjustment.

The molded fiber glass technique is used effectively in these signs and points out the potential design freedom available to designers using this process.

5. U.S. Border Station
San Diego, California/Region 9

Actual Evaluation: From a design standpoint, the system is successful. From a functional and cost standpoint, it is not. The border station appears to be overdone with signs. "Law Enforcement" appears too many times. The color does not work well with the architecture inside or out.

Unit costs are so prohibitive that locally supplied substitutes, which can be obtained in a much shorter time and at reasonable costs, are being sought. There is no flexibility at all in the signs.

There are numerous routed signs throughout the border station which apparently were not included in the contract, but in fact contain some of the most important information.

The biggest problem is that the signs do not control traffic, particularly pedestrian. People just don't read them.

This project was coordinated from GSA's central office in Washington, D.C. There appears to have been a lack of communication concerning specific building needs and consideration of system perpetuation and replacement.

6. Federal Building—U.S. Courthouse
San Diego, California/Region 9

Actual Evaluation: This project is the most successful system researched. It provides the necessary flexibility for change with in-house processes which reduce time and cost. The system is total in providing both uniformity of design of all elements and being coordinated and implemented thoroughly throughout the building. All aspects of this system design and materials project a high level of quality.

Surprisingly, this project was designed and produced in an extremely compressed time schedule. To achieve this, all parties involved maintained close communication.

This is the only system of the 10 which utilizes dark copy on light background. This obviously was to conform to constraints of the varitype system of producing message strips. The results are successful.

The one weakness in the system is the use of special snap devices to fasten message strip holders to sign frames. The bonding material is less than desirable.

7. SSA Regional Program Centers
Philadelphia, Pennsylvania/
Region 3
Richmond, California/Region9

Actual Evluation: From a design standpoint, the system is successful. Generally all of the information needs are satisfied. One negative point concerning graphic application is the use of surface-applied color and graphics. This was done to conform to the exterior sign system but is considered less than desirable when compared to the subsurface processes.

There were two major problems with this project. First, the same criteria were set up for both buildings. This turned out to be a problem because both building tenants did not, in fact, operate identically, despite being the same federal agency. The second problem deals with GSA in Washington setting guidelines for the project, with minimum input from GSA regional personnel and tenants.

Both of these problems led to oversimplification of actual tenant needs and eventual inadequacies in the system dealing with changeability.

There were a number of deficiencies in the finished signs which required attention. The contractor failed to provide a maintenace and replacement outline to the tenant, although this was required in the specifications. As a result, improper maintenance procedures were used on some items, which caused further damage. SSA management attempted to acquire assistance without success. Neither GSA nor the contractor responded appropriately.

The designer was requested to assist in solving this problem. Simply by assembling representatives from each party concerned at the site in Richmond, the problems were identified and appropriate corrective measures were initiated. If coordination between GSA and SSA had been more thorough, this problem likely would not have occurred.

8. Federal Building
Chicago, Illinois/Region 5

Actual Evluation: Apparently an attempt was made to use color coding; however, the variation of two shades of brown is so subtle that the result seems to be more a material color mismatch than its intended function.

Routed messages are used which are graphically less than adequate. They are, however, being replaced with die-cut vinyl letters.

Many of the signs are held in place magnetically. Others are bonded onto plastic frames. The paper base phenolic materials used under the original contract have severely warped to the point of falling off their mounts. This results in more than 50 percent of all signs not being used; they were consequently stored. A replacement material is now being used which has a rubber base and will not warp. Die-cut vinyl is used for message application. This will provide greater flexibility for change with less wasted material.

Many of the signs are ceiling-hung and perpendicular to traffic flow. Consequently they require double-face signs. The custom hangers and frames appear less than adequate.

9. Federal Building—U.S. Courthouse
Portland, Oregon/Region 10

Actual Evaluation: This project is quite adequate and seems to meet the requirements of the tenants successfully. While changeability is handled by an outside source, it seems to be workable for the building's management. There is a local supplier who is geared to this system and who responds sufficiently.

This system is a good example of a successfully implemented and administered system utilizing standard materials and processes.

10. Federal Building—U.S. Courthouse
Topeka, Kansas/Region 6

Actual Evaluation: This system is a departure from most other projects researched. There is no use of acrylic materials. Instead, painted wood and hardboard are used with die-cut vinyl graphics.

Building management is satisfied with the system and does not foresee problems with changeability.

Supergraphics are used very effectively throughout the parking and court areas.

ASSESSMENT SUMMARY

From evaluation of the demonstration projects, a definite pattern of information emerges which suggests an assessment that can be applied generally. These are related to the categories of evaluation questions and the information gathered in each of those categories.

1. Relevant Criteria

While it can be said that most of the systems satisfied project requirements, it should be pointed out that in most cases, GSA set the requirements that the tenant would receive. The tenant mainly provided message input. A number of systems broke down because of absence of certain types of signs, which forced the tenant to provide for temporary needs. Thus, temporary substitutes became permanent items.

Most systems minimally controlled and assisted the users. Those that did not control were incomplete, and not through a lack of good design. This points to the fact that the system approach in each case was sufficient. Inadequate implementation and follow-through caused the system's breakdown.

Extensive amounts of money were paid to professional design consultants to develop appropriate signage systems. Through a lack of proper input to the designers in some cases, and the absence of system perpetuation in others, a number of projects were not effectively utilized.

When appropriate guidelines and systems are developed, it is imperative that proper planning, funding, and follow-through be maintained. If the systems cannot be controlled using professional consultants, there is little chance for improvement if the systems are developed by in-house staff alone.

In observing visitors to various buildings, it became apparent that a large majority do not read lengthy signs. In fact, many people do not read signs at all, but proceed in confusion until they ask someone how to reach a certain place. This points to the need for a simplified systems approach to signs, keeping messages brief, readable, and well located.

2. Economic Soundness

To say that each project was obtained within its budget is correct but misleading, since budget limits were relatively undefined and the low bid was always taken.

Based on today's standards throughout the sign industry, the majority of the systems are not considered costly. Most of them utilize acrylic material with subsurface applied graphics. These materials and processes are expensive in comparison to other less desirable methods. Unless one can standardize components and maintain low cost in-house, or outside sources, for messages, where the one-of-a-kind sign can be produced inexpensively, unit costs are going to be high.

Installation costs are relatively constant as long as the signs are to be wall-mounted. Special freestanding, ceiling-hung, and flagged signs depart from the routine foam-tape or adhesive-mounting techniques, and will certainly involve higher installation costs.

3. Compliance with Special Requirements

Local codes and ordinances primarily affect exterior site signs and are not to be considered a factor of constraint. Codes should be adhered to for building identification.

No provisions for the visually handicapped were made in any of the projects researched. The general conclusion is that to make suitable provisions for the visually handicapped, which constitutes a very small number of visitors, is not practical or economically feasible. Research has been conducted to determine what would constitute adequate provisions for the blind. Raised letters as opposed to braille are better, since most blind people became blind at some time later than birth, and many of these people cannot read braille. Some elevator manufacturers are now including provisions for the blind in the elevator controls.

While emergency evacuation information is required in federal buildings, only a few projects gave any consideration to providing this information. This is because it is costly to reproduce multiple floor plans through regular production methods compatible with sign systems. There is also the element of change which, in large buildings, could affect numerous signs on a single floor. Uniform guidelines need to be established for the use of these items, and they should be standardized from building to building in their function and locations.

Due to the amount of work required to prepare floor plans and reproduce them, a number of buildings simply have photocopy paper marked in pen for emergency evacuation plans. This is another segment of a system's breakdown because of oversight or cost constraint.

4. Flexibility

Changeability is necessary and frequent. The degree and frequency vary with different components and different facilities. The three most common items of change are directories, room identification, and special-information signs. If individual names are used in the system, this increases the need for change because personnel changes occur more frequently than room-function changes.

Unfortunately, most systems reviewed do not lend themselves to ease of change. This does not refer to access to the changeable component of the sign, but rather to access to procurement of the changeable element. Only two systems actually utilize in-house capabilities for changeable information production. Yet this provides the most time-saving, efficient, and least expensive method of change. It should be made clear that this does not include providing the total sign, but only the changeable letter strip. Both the varitype and Letteron die-cut vinyl methods are effective and inexpensive, even considering the initial equipment investment.

Total flexibility would be achieved if both messages and background color were readily changeable for those items specifically needing changeability. Standardization of sizes of units within a certain sign type is necessary to simplify inventory and production.

A very important conclusion drawn from all of the evaluations is that no system or office should be put in the position of having to rely on an extended in-house skill for maintaining changeability within a system. The method must be as self-sufficient as possible and still conform to design guidelines.

5. Durability

For the most part, signs using acrylic materials with subsurface applied graphics are most serviceable and durable. Signs with frames are generally more susceptible to problems of warping or delamination. While frames will generally incur additional cost, they may be a vehicle to satisfy mass-produced component assembly and changeability.

Routed signs are least desirable despite potential in-house capabilities of production. Like subsurface applied messages, once made they are permanent and not changeable.

While acrylics are commonly acceptable today, other materials such as metal could be appropriate if component-assembled units were used.

Generally, materials used throughout these systems perform appropriately for their intended use.

6. Antivandalism

In every instance, vandalism did not appear to be a significant factor. However, those systems with changeable strips which were not captured were most susceptible to removal. It is appropriate to consider that in most instances, any resistance to quick removal is a sufficient deterrent. Both employees and visitors can be vandals.

7. Replacement

Most sign companies would rather not bother with replacement orders unless the quantity is substantial. There are a few who offer well-organized ordering systems for various sign components. One company has actually computerized its order system to reduce cost and turnaround time. Message strip replacement is more accessible providing it uses a photographic or silk-screened process.

For the most part, building or tenant management should be able to plan ahead for 10 days' to 2 weeks' turnaround time. However, there is nothing more accessible than producing the sign or sign changes immediately. The relationship of time to need is a factor to contend with.

Replacement items will have less chance of being compatible with the original system as time passes due to lack of control of raw materials, paint match, and varying conditions from one supplier to another in the event of supplier change. It is strongly recommended that a reasonable supply of sign blanks and related components be included with the original contract order to cover predictable needs.

8. Repairability

Most acrylic signs with subsurface applied graphics are not repairable. It is most feasible to order a new sign. Some molded glass-fiber-reinforced exterior signs can be repaired but color match is a problem. A component-assembled sign using interchangeable parts would reduce sign fatality by allowing only the damaged part to be replaced. Delaminations and loosened joints can be repaired.

From discussions with various sign suppliers, repair is not practical unless it is minimal and can be done on site. Replacement is just as fast. Of course, a determining factor is the extent of damage and how the signs are fabricated.

9. Fabricator Adaptability

Today, the sign industry is much more sophisticated than it was just a few years ago. Most reputable sign companies can produce the majority of architectural sign systems, including exterior and interior. Most of these companies can adapt to system uniqueness within reasonable limits, certainly within the practical limits of signs for most requirements.

Unit costs are a necessary item and will, no doubt, become more significant as times passes.

Suppliers should be called upon to update and clearly define their processes and newly developed technology continuously in order to maintain a constant awareness of the state of the art in the sign industry. Standardization of certain common processes should be required among qualified sign companies to allow effective use of performance specifications.

10. Security

Sign systems, for the most part, are not a significant factor in maintaining security in a building.

11. Color

Color coding has not been used successfully in any of the demonstration projects. The need was not sufficient to warrant its use. Color coding should not, however, be denied consideration. Color is an important element in any sign system. It can be a lively element in contrast to a mundane environment. It can also be neutral and subtle. Color plays an important role in the communication characteristic of a sign system.

In most cases, colors used were minimally compatible with the architecture. Bronze backgrounds were quite common.

Only one project used color as a subtle background—light, with dark copy. This minimizes the impact of a color area or patch occurring from place to place on walls. This may well be desirable. The reverse is also appropriate—dark background, with contrasting light copy. This suggests the desirability of color option selectivity, from one functional area to another.

Lighting and mounting surface color will be significant factors in determining the use of color. Color use should be controlled and limited to a certain professionally determined range of colors and uses.

12. Lighting

Federal energy conservation requirements are the single most critical constraints which effect sign systems. Many of the systems reviewed were less than effective due to reduced light levels in buildings. This will, no doubt, affect future system design and the use of color and positive/negative background and copy relationships.

Other than certain directory units, integral illumination is not practical for interior signs (except exit signs). Considering that most federal buildings are closed after 5 P.M., illumination for exterior signs should be optional and determined at the local level. External illumination is more economical than integral illumination within a sign, but less desirable.

13. Mounting

Most of the systems used double-sided foam tape and/or silicone adhesives. Unless the adhesive is carefully removed by using a thin wire to cut it, damage to painted or vinyl-covered walls is almost sure to occur. Use of the wire will allow the adhesive to be separated and removed from both the back of the sign and the mounting surface. If the sign has subsurface graphics or color on the back, damage may occur to the sign if the wire is used. A better method for mounting or standardization of mounting units or frames should be developed. Ideally, a sign should be sufficiently changeable to eliminate the need to remove the sign at all. Removal damage effect is lessened if another sign of similar size replaces the one removed. Nevertheless, changeable components would tend to eliminate these problems.

14. Size

Most of the signs were sufficient in size. However, there was a variety of formats, sizes, and typefaces utilized within a single system and, in some cases, an individualized sign. Excessive amounts of information was not a major factor but, in some cases, the use of a simple format for determining message-length limits for signs would have prevented most of the awkward layout situations.

It is apparent that some systems did not accommodate or take into account certain message requirements, as indicated by a variety of tacked-on appendages containing additional information.

15. Sign Message Information

Room numbering was widely used and is important. Standardization in room numbering is difficult because of varying building designs. Existing buildings can be modified to a standard system. Architects for future facilities should be instructed to work within a standard format.

Symbols are used in just about every project and with an equal number of different interpretations. For the most part, actual use or variations of the DOT symbol signs were used.

Following are some additional conclusions drawn from evaluation activities.

There were frequent attempts to incorporate various agency seals into signs. There does not appear to be any standard for which seals are to be used by the agencies, especially those with more than one seal, nor is there a simple method for obtaining reproducible art for approved seals.

Generally, there was a negative attitude that overshadowed a number of these projects that dealt with tenant/building management relationships. Tenants felt that they were dictated by the landlord/manager when determining their needs. Also, communication among central office, regional office (GSA), and local management with tenants was less than efficient.

It seems practical to assume that while strict adherence to most professional graphic-design guidelines is desirable (and, indeed, necessary) for optimum system design, certain compromises should be considered as valid trade-offs in order to achieve desirable system flexibilities which, in the long term, will benefit more substantially than rigid adherence to any one set of guidelines.

The scope and design of a building information system suggest the potential introduction of supergraphics where applicable as a functional/aesthetic aspect of the built environment.

Supergraphics is not to be considered a subsystem, but rather a medium by which subsystem components are presented. It is necessary to approach the use of supergraphics strictly on an individual project basis, as the application and scale of supergraphics is unique for each facility.

It is recommended that phasing of sign-system implementation not be considered beyond exterior/interior and facility/tenant function separation.

Because of the varied complexities of needs and functions which comprise the built environment, the designer must be concerned with total visual communications problems, and not just with solving individual sign needs. Looking at these problems from a systems approach with the intention of satisfying as many of the existing functional/aesthetic requirements as possible within its framework is the best approach.

Tying Down Some Loose Ends

"Cost effectiveness" and "efficiency" are watchwords that equate time with money and are common to all commercial enterprises. It is logical to assume, therefore, that any device which serves to reduce performance time and cuts costs will find ready acceptance at all levels of management. The following recommendations regarding technical proposal procedures are a distillation of comments and suggestions expressed by many environmental graphic designers and, although principally directed to federal government agencies, should also prove valuable to any who are concerned with acquiring environmental graphic design services.

1. Solicitation forms should not be items that have been adapted from forms normally used for cost proposals obtained from building or manufacturing contractors, because the designer is a professional providing services rather than goods.

2. Detailed information concerning project requirements should be provided, such as: Are code signs to be included? Are exterior signs included? Are all signs nonilluminated?

   In order to determine the exact scope of work, the designer must provide or be provided with precise information as to the following: How many types of signs are required? What quantities of signs in each type are desired? What are the planned locations of signs?

   This information can be determined only after the designer has analyzed architectural plans and planned all signing and graphic requirements for the entire project. This is normally considered the first phase of any signage design project.

3. If a design firm is to be selected on the basis of overall design ability, and not merely on its ability to fill out forms correctly, the firm should be required to submit slides, photographs, or other visual documentation of past design work for evaluation.

4. There is no way of accurately determining cost or fee requirements for any large job before it has been analyzed and the entire program planned.

5. Where fee proposals vary widely, this suggests that some of the bidders are not clear about the scope of work and are "guesstimating."

   Also, this might indicate that the various designers solicited had entirely different kinds of systems in mind. One designer might plan to use "off the shelf" components, while another might plan a custom system to solve both functional and aesthetic problems in an ideal way. Designing the latter requires much higher fees than the former. Unless the buyer specifies which approach is required, the designer may use the most expedient approach.

6. To ensure that the designer who is best qualified to provide the buyer's requirements is competitively selected, the following suggestions are made:
   a. Evaluation of the design firm's qualifications should include a review of slides or other visual material submitted by them.
   b. At least one member of the team which evaluates graphic design proposals should be a designer capable of evaluating the visual material submitted.
   c. A copy of the evaluation should be returned to the unsuccessful designers after a selection has been made, to help them improve their performance on future proposals.
   d. A cross-referenced file could be established which rates qualified designers according to specific design ability, past performance, size of staff, location, and so forth.
   e. From this file three to five firms whose qualifications fit the requirements of the project could be selected to submit a proposal for the first phase, consisting of predesign analysis and planning.
   f. Depending on the nature of the project, one of the following procedures should be used:
      (1.) The best-qualified firm should be selected to proceed on a cost-plus basis on the first phase.
      (2.) If, on a specific project, competitive bidding is required, then three or more sign firms could submit proposals covering only the first phase.

7. By evaluating the first-phase fee proposals of these firms, the buyer can select one firm with which to proceed. The first-phase study would define the preliminary scope of work, quantity and placement of signs, and so forth, Upon completion of the first phase, with the scope clearly defined, the design firm can submit a lump-sum fee proposal covering all the remaining phases of work. Or, as a double check, the buyer can get proposals from additional firms at this point, based on the scope of work determined by the first-phase study.

8. Along with the first-phase fee proposal, which should average 10 percent of the total fee, the design firm should also submit a statement defining the kind of sign system to be provided, i.e., (1) a custom-designed system, (2) a mix of custom-designed elements and modified "off

the shelf" items, or (3) a system composed solely of "off the shelf" items.

9. The federal government should consider using the method and language employed in the solicitation/negotiation for architectural services. This would solve most of the problems encountered in the acquisition of environmental graphic-design services. However, it is the professional graphic-design community, not the government agencies, that should instigate this change.

The law covering the federal government's solicitation of architectural services is P.L. 92.582, Selection of Architects and Engineers. It is this law that needs to be amended to include the professional environmental graphics designer.

To support this action, demonstrated qualifications critical to recognition and acceptance as a separate professional design entity should be fully documented and channeled, as a request for official recognition and inclusion in the "process," to the proper parties of the U.S. Congress.

In the process of achieving this end, other significant benefits will certainly accrue to both government and commercial clients, as well as to the professionals who serve them.

Notes and Bibliography

CHAPTER OPENING CREDITS

Preface: Quotation, Gabriel Garcia Marquez, from *One Hundred Years of Solitude*.

Foreword: by Dave Meyer of Dave Meyer & Associates.

Chapter 1: Quotation, Oscar Wilde, historical data on alphabets drawn from *Illustrated World Encyclopedia*, 1 volume edition, Boblly Publishing Corp., Woodbury, N.Y., 1977, pp. 78, 79.

Chapter 2: Quotation, Dr. Karl Pribram, professor of psychology, Stanford University, Stanford, Calif. Sign classification symbol coding from GSA Bilingual Graphic Communications System for U.S. Border Stations Manual. Semiotic definition from DOT-OS-40192. November 1974 symbol-signs.

Chapter 3: Quotation, Peter Gorb, from introduction to "Living by Design"—Pentagram. Market evaluation, Stanley Bloom, ASI, Marina Del Ray, Calif., in a talk to NESA conference, Mar. 27, 1979.

Chapter 4: Quotation, Nicollette Gray in *AIA Journal*, October 1975, p. 35.

Chapter 5: Quotation, Paul Arthur, RCA, Newton, Frank, Arthur, Toronto, Canada. Letter forms quotations; Paul Standard and T. M. Cledand, taken from Herman Zapf's *Manuale Typographicum*. Reference to British Underground Rail and Heathrow Airport system's alphabets from Crosby/Fletcher/Forbes, *A Sign Systems Manual*, Praeger Publishers, New York, 1970. "X-height" reference material from Federal Identity Program (FIP) Signage Standards, The Treasury Board of Canada. Light source (illumination) data derived, in part, from SEGD's *Environmental Graphics Sourcebook*, Part One.

Chapter 6: Quotation, Lawrence K. Frank, in an essay "The World Is a Communications Network" for the book *Sign, Image, Symbol*, George Braziller, New York, 1966. Design guidelines for symbols and symbol/signs are condensed and edited from material originated by Paul Arthur for the U.S. General Services Administration.

Incidental modifications, made in the interest of system conformity, have in no way changed the original concept or design intent.

Chapter 7: Catalog of signs was adapted from material developed for GSA by Dave Meyer & Associates. Summary of materials and techniques is condensed from part of SEGD's *Environmental Graphics Sourcebook*, Part One. Note: The *Sourcebook*, in three parts, is being produced in cooperation with NESA.

Chapter 8: Quotation, A. Eddington, in "The Nature of Physics." "A/E Selection and Award Network" and "The Procurement Cycle" are from GSA. "Client Guide for Signage and Architectural Graphics" is by the Michigan Council for the Arts. The detailed flow chart was developed by John R. Berry for Smith, Hynchman & Grylls Associates, Inc.

Chapter 9: Design intent drawings were adapted from original material by Dave Meyer & Associates for GSA's signage standards.

Chapter 10: Technical specifications were adapted from original material by Dave Meyer & Associates for GSA's signage standards.

Appendix: Quotation, William Gowers, Chapter 19 of *The Brain: The Last Frontier* by Richard M. Restak, M.D., Doubleday, 1979. Digest of the data base was adapted from Evaluation of Ten Federal Building Sign System Demonstration Projects by Dave Meyer & Associates, for GSA. "Loose ends," derived from a letter by John Follis of JF&A. Others whose ideas and philosophies have become so inextricably mixed with those of the authors as to make blame or credit impossible are:
Jich Burns
Jeffry Corbin
Michael J. Davis
Colin Forbes
David M. Souder

BIBLIOGRAPHY

Crosby/Fletcher/Forbes, *A Sign System Manual* (1970), Praeger Publishers, 521 Fifth Avenue, New York, NY 10017

Henry Dreyfuss: *Symbol Sourcebook* (1972), McGraw-Hill Book Company, 1221 Avenue of the Americas, New York, NY 10020

Evans, Ralph M.: *An Introduction to Color* (1948), John Wiley & Sons, Inc., 605 Third Avenue, New York, NY 10158

Follis, John, and Dave Hammer: *Architectural Signing & Graphics* (1979), Whitney Library of Design, 1515 Broadway, New York, NY 10036

Graves, Maitland: *The Art of Color and Design* (1951),McGraw-Hill Book Company 1221 Avenue of the Americas, New York, NY 10020

Judd & Kelley: *Color—Universal Language and Dictionary of Names* (1976), NBS special publication #440, stock #003-003-01705-1, U.S. Government Printing Office, 1710 North Capitol Street, N.W., Washington, DC 20402

National Technical Information Service: *Symbol Signs*, DOT-OS-40192, November 1974, and *Symbol Signs 2*, DOT-OS-60510, March 1979, Springfield, VA 22151

Society of Environmental Graphics Designers: *Environmental Graphics Sourcebook* (1978); 2200 Bridgeway Boulevard, Sausalito, California 94965

U.S. Government Printing Office: *Manual on Uniform Traffic Control Devices*, stock #050-001-8100-8, 1710 North Capitol Street, N.W., Washington, DC 20402

Whitney Library of Design: *Living by Design—Pentagram* (1978), 1515 Broadway, New York, NY 10036

Write for book lists from technical libraries of:

Institute of Signage Research, 4020 Fabian Way, Palo Alto, CA 94304

NESA, Suite 310E, 2625 Butterfield Road, Oak Brook, IL 60521

ST Publications, 407 Gilbert Avenue, Cincinnati, OH 45202

For information on doing business with the U.S. General Services Administration (GSA), Public Building Service, contact the business services office of the GSA regional office for your area. Addresses by region and the states included are:

GSA Region 1 John W. McCormack Post Office and Courthouse, Boston, MA 02109
(Maine, New Hampshire, Vermont, Massachusetts, Rhode Island, Connecticut)

GSA Region 2: 26 Federal Plaza, New York, NY 10007
(New York, New Jersey, Puerto Rico, Virgin Islands)

GSA Region 3: GSA Regional Office Building, 7th and D Streets, S.W., Washington, DC 20407
(Washington, D.C., Maryland, Virginia, West Virginia, Pennsylvania)

GSA Region 4: 1776 Peachtree Street, N.W., Atlanta, GA 30309
(North Carolina, South Carolina, Georgia, Florida, Alabama, Mississippi, Tennessee, Kentucky)

GSA Region 5: John C. Kluczynski Federal Building, 230 South Dearboard Street, Chicago, IL 60604
(Minnesota, Ohio, Indiana, Michigan, Wisconsin, Illinois)

GSA Region 6: Federal Building, 1500 East Bannister Road, Kansas City, MO 64131
(Iowa, Kansas, Missouri, Nebraska)

GSA Region 7: 819 Taylor Street, Fort Worth, TX 76102
(Texas, Oklahoma, Louisiana, Arkansas, New Mexico)

GSA Region 8: Building 41, Denver Federal Center, Denver CO 80225
(Montana, North and South Dakota, Colorado, Wyoming, Utah)

GSA Region 9: 525 Market Street, San Francisco, CA 94105
(California, Nevada, Hawaii, Arizona, Guam, trust territory of the Pacific)

GSA Region 10: GSA Center, Auburn, WA 98002
(Washington, Oregon, Idaho, Alaska)

Acronym Glossary

AIGA   American Institute of Graphic Arts
ANSI   American National Standards Institute
BOMA   Building Owners and Managers Association International
BRAB   Building Research Advisory Board
DOT   Department of Transportation
GPO   Government Printing Office
GSA   General Services Administration
ISO   International Organization for Standardization
NBS   National Bureau of Standards
NEII   National Elevator Industry, Inc.
NESA   National Electric Sign Association
OSHA   Occupational Safety and Health Administration
SEGD   Society of Environmental Graphics Designers
ST   Signs of the Times

Index